About the Author

Phenomenologist Stephen Lancaster (North Carolina) has been involved in the field of paranormal research since 1997, conducting investigative work for politicians, military facilities, the board of education, museums, commercial locations, businesses, television, and civilian properties. His research is recognized by the US government. He has appeared on NBC Universal's *Shocking... Scary... Paranormal Videos*, A&E Biography's *My Ghost Story*, and Travel Channel's *A Haunting*. Stephen also appears in *Fantôme: The Haunting of Brentwood Wine Bistro*, a paranormal documentary revolving around the most haunted restaurant in the world. Visit him online at facebook.com /authorstephenlancaster.

The TRUE STORY of a
POSSESSED DOLL'S REVENGE

STEPHEN LANCASTER

Llewellyn Worldwide
Woodbury, Minnesota

FIRST EDITION
First Printing, 2020

Cover design by Shira Atakpu
Editing by Hanna Grimson
Interior photos provided by the author

Llewellyn Publications is a registered trademark of Llewellyn Worldwide Ltd.

Library of Congress Cataloging-in-Publication Data
Names: Lancaster, Stephen,
Title: Norman 2 : the true story of a possessed doll's revenge / Stephen
  Lancaster.
Description: [Woodbury, Minnesota] : Llewellyn Publications, [2020] |
  Includes bibliographical references. | Summary: "Norman 2 chronicles the
  further attacks of Norman the haunted doll on the Lancaster family after
  the events of Norman. From setting himself and the barn on fire to
  injuring the family dog, Norman is determined to terrorize Stephen and
  his family. As the haunting gets worse, Stephen is forced to accept that
  something must be done to stop Norman permanently"—Provided by
  publisher.
Identifiers: LCCN 2020020870 (print) | LCCN 2020020871 (ebook) | ISBN
  9780738766072 (paperback) | ISBN 9780738766232 (ebook)
Subjects: LCSH: Norman (Doll) | Parapsychology. | Dolls—Miscellanea.
Classification: LCC BF1439 .L363 2020 (print) | LCC BF1439 (ebook) | DDC
  130—dc23
LC record available at https://lccn.loc.gov/2020020870
LC ebook record available at https://lccn.loc.gov/2020020871

Llewellyn Worldwide Ltd. does not participate in, endorse, or have any authority or responsibility concerning private business transactions between our authors and the public.

All mail addressed to the author is forwarded but the publisher cannot, unless specifically instructed by the author, give out an address or phone number.

Any internet references contained in this work are current at publication time, but the publisher cannot guarantee that a specific location will continue to be maintained. Please refer to the publisher's website for links to authors' websites and other sources.

Llewellyn Publications
A Division of Llewellyn Worldwide Ltd.
2143 Wooddale Drive
Woodbury, MN 55125-2989
www.llewellyn.com

Printed in the United States of America

Contents

Disclaimer

I have tried to recreate events, locales, and conversations from my memories of them. In order to maintain their anonymity in some instances, I have changed the names of individuals and places, and I may have changed some identifying characteristics and details such as physical properties, occupations, and places of residence.

The following literary work contains graphic and intense situations, coarse language, factual paranormal events, unsettling photographs, and gruesome incidents involving animals. Please read with this in mind and review before allowing any person under the age of seventeen to read.

Dedication

This book is dedicated to my loving wife, Christina. We've seen what most dream of.

Foreword

When I wrote the foreword for this book's predecessor in 2018, Mr. Lancaster had documented Norman the doll for well over a year.

Stephen and I met nearly thirteen years ago at a paranormal conference in Virginia. Our friendship blossomed over the years as we helped one another out with various undisclosed cases and projects. One project in particular was of course the "Norman" case, or as Stephen initially dubbed it, "the evil *objet d'art.*"

Haunted objects have always been a fascination of mine, so when I was approached by a credible researcher such as Stephen with a potentially haunted doll, my ears perked up. A haunted doll is typically a homemade, handmade, or even a manufactured doll or stuffed toy that is reportedly possessed by an evil entity or cursed in some fashion.

The origin of haunted dolls dates back to ancient Egypt where the enemies of Ramesses III used wax figures and images of his likeness to murder him supernaturally. In the present day, the origins of haunted dolls vary. A soul that refused to carry on can sometimes be transferred to an object or what we label as a toy.

Sentimental reasoning or even personal fondness for an item can result in a spirit becoming attached to any particular component. In certain religious sects, it is believed one can bind a spirit to an object, trapping it for timeless existence.

Admittedly, I was skeptical when Stephen initially approached me about the haunted doll. His claims were unrestrained and exceedingly difficult to digest considering I had yet to witness anything to coincide with the subject matter.

I requested to see the surveillance footage and anything else Mr. Lancaster had concerning Norman before I agreed to write the previous foreword and any others that may follow. Upon viewing, I was shocked to see a rarity in the paranormal field. Honestly, the footage of Norman moving his head was one of the best pieces of paranormal evidence in favor of haunted objects existing I had ever seen.

In the most telling video, Norman moves his head and does so in a fashion that is physically impossible. The doll was not manufactured to allow its head to look down. Yet in the video he does. His eyes also turned completely black. This was unsettling and very telling.

The spirit inside of the doll was evil by nature.

I remember viewing this clip dozens of times, and every time I did, chills went down my spine. The amount of intelligence conveyed was surprising at first.

To the highest degree, Mr. Lancaster truly had in his possession one of the most haunted dolls I have ever witnessed in my life. I have followed Stephen's research on Norman ever since. But I wasn't the only one. Stephen also sought out the opinion of demonologist, ZoZologist, and innovator Darren Evans.

In 2019, alongside Mr. Lancaster and his wife, Darren would take the research a step forward after conducting a personal communication session with Norman a year after I reviewed the captivating footage. Originally, I was to be there. The three paranormal researchers were in Virginia filming for the Travel Channel's *A Haunting*. I was to be interviewed as well for the show concerning Norman, but scheduling conflicts and health issues prevented me from doing as much.

As I am sure you will read in the pages that follow, they stumbled upon something even more powerful with the doll. They filmed an investigation into Norman at their hotel with captivating results. That video received thousands upon thousands of views on social media and stunned the audience.

The more we learned about Norman, the wearier I became being involved. I told both Stephen and Darren that I would be stepping back from the darkness that Norman was producing. I felt in my heart that researching him further was a mistake.

I was cautious and warned the both of them of the repercussions of opening that doll's heart even further. What happened in the months to follow validated that I was right in believing the ghost of Norman is the blackest of souls.

Haunted dolls exist. I have seen it for myself, and there certainly isn't one like Norman.

He's special.

—Rosemary Ellen Guiley

Rosemary Ellen Guiley (1950–2019) was one of the leading experts in the paranormal with more than sixty-seven books to her credit. With John Zaffis, she coauthored two books on haunted objects: *Haunted by the Things You Love* (2014) and *Demon Haunted: True Stories from the John Zaffis Vault* (2016).

Preface

Flare and flame flew from his eye as the horrific and immoral entity within attempted to break free from his impressionable cloth shell. In an amazing defiance of all known physics, the power and burning wickedness singed not his body. For only his eye revealed the menacing darkness desperate to feed on the fearful living once more.

The Trojan horse was formally animate again and no longer content with the confines of his infantile prison. In fact, I refuse to believe he ever was. The creature had grown impatient, and that point was made perfectly clear through his act of desperation.

Peace in our world ceased exactly one year this Christmas past. His fire and wrath were finally unleashed on us. There was no other alternative. I had to open the damned door.

In the summer of 2016, my fiancée and I acquired a unique and mischievous looking doll from a local antique shop. The entire situation of purchasing him was a conundrum, to say the least.

The two old women working the shop were very hesitant at first to tell us much about him. Although they did confide a backstory that consisted of a house burning to the ground with the mother of a young girl dying in the fire. The young girl survived the tragic event, but she wasn't the only one. She was able to save her only friend—a doll manufactured by Mattel—called Matty.

The doll had been given as a gift at the hospital at the time of her birth. She was to have a twin brother but, sadly, he passed away in the womb. Matty became this young girl's missing brother.

However, something supernatural attached itself to the doll that day at the hospital. Matty became an evil, possessed doll that wreaked havoc wherever he went. His aim always seemed to target male figures or those that knew his secret. I believe to this day that the entity inside of the doll held a grudge of some sort.

The young girl grew up and kept the doll as, what I believe to be, the only memory she had left of the family that once was. Decades later, as an unmarried adult, she would walk into that very same antique shop and give the doll away. The reasoning behind that still remains a mystery.

Before we finally purchased the doll, the one old woman made sure to tell me that she believed the doll came directly from hell. Needless to say, as a paranormal researcher, I didn't think much of it. We just wanted to add the doll to our already vast collection of vintage and antique items. The backstory certainly added an intoxicating allure to owning the doll. He just seemed to be a perfect fit considering my fiancée and I were, and still are, paranormal researchers.

In retrospect, I believe the old woman was very close to the truth. If not hell, he came from a place with pure evil attached.

I wasted no time renaming the doll Norman because he just didn't come across as normal to me. He didn't sit right with us from the start. There was something definitely abnormal about him. I felt it in my gut.

It didn't take long after we brought the old doll into our home for strange activity to start taking place. At first it was subtle and nearly dismissible. But it escalated over time to a point beyond my family's comfort zone.

In the beginning, phantom knocks would be heard throughout our house. It was common to hear objects being moved or for unpredictable power outages to occur. There were even instances of mechanical failure across some of our household electrical devices.

However, much of what occurred in the very beginning, I easily dismissed as a product of one of our many household pets. Never did I think a haunted doll was the culprit. But my views quickly changed when the activity went from playful to vengeful and damaging.

The intensifying activity led to infestations of insects like flies and spiders, rats, and even a snake. These were infestations that even an exterminator could not explain.

Once we were fully convinced our house was being haunted by the doll, we started paying more attention to our home surveillance. We discovered him on more than one occasion moving on his own and even placing my grandchild in a trance.

Having the home-field advantage when dealing with something paranormal was something both my fiancée and I jumped right on. We saw it as a great opportunity to research a truly haunted object. But when lives became threatened and endangered, our tune changed.

The supernatural activity escalated to the point that my entire family was living in fear. Norman haunted my soon-to-be stepdaughter by writing messages on a mirror and causing chaos when she attempted to sleep.

He started throwing objects at me and sending messages through our phone and computer. The doll could maneuver as an invisible force, randomly shoving me to the ground. On one specifically scary day, the entity inside of Norman caused me to have a heart attack.

Tragically, he also killed one of our animals. I discovered my cat had been murdered, and it was done in such a way that nothing rational could explain it.

During Hurricane Matthew, we even captured an image of the entity himself. He was dark and foreboding and everything you could imagine something terrifying and monstrous would be.

His actions led us to believe that he was looking to replace what he should have had if he had survived childbirth. I am leaning strongly toward believing the doll is possessed by the stillborn child's spirit. The mounting evidence nearly landslides in favor of that belief. He wanted a family, and he wanted it to be just like the old lady's story at the antique shop. Norman wanted that mother and that sister, and he wanted my fiancée and her daughter as their replacements.

I firmly believe the mother from the old story became suspicious of the doll's possessed nature. The fire that killed her was most likely a direct result of that knowledge. We couldn't allow the same thing to happen to us since the doll was fully aware we knew what he was.

My fiancée and I were forced to make a decision. We had acquired more than enough evidence to prove Norman was haunted. With our home no longer feeling like a safe place, we had to take action. But that was easier said than done.

You can't just throw away a ghost. Nobody has that power. You also cannot destroy a ghost. That's why destroying the doll was never really a considered option. Spiritual binding or protection can take place and is often practiced, but that does not vanquish the entity. Those methods simply protect you from the undesired spirit.

Consider the famous Annabelle doll locked away in the Warrens' Occult Museum. It is believed that doll is extremely haunted. But the spirit inside could not be destroyed. The best the Warrens could do was lock the doll away in a glass case to prevent any further supernatural activity because they believed that destroying the doll only removed the vessel.

Then there is Robert, the doll who is firmly sealed in a museum in Florida. His possession is so believed, the museum refuses to allow anybody to touch him. Like Annabelle, he spends his existence barred behind glass.

In our case, we locked Norman away in his own room. But even that had consequences. We were dealing with the paranormal and elements that cannot be explained scientifically. So it was a shot in the dark to even attempt it.

We felt that the entity inside of Norman was looking for some semblance of a normal, childhood life. Our previous research led us to believe that the twin boy who died in the early 1960s was actually the spirit inside the vintage doll. If that was the case, he missed out on everything life had to offer. That would explain his disdain for the living and his obsession with finding a replacement family.

We converted an old room in our house into a children's bedroom where Norman would be placed and stored until we were forced to relocate him. The room was sealed and monitored and, for the time being, the remainder of our house went back to normal.

I don't think there is a specific scientific, medical definition for anxiety that never goes away. I write this with my right leg bouncing vigorously. Reliving everything again to tell you the story isn't as easy as it may seem.

Norman died in 1962 yet was born after his death. Wrap your head around that mind-bender. He came into our home. He came into our lives. He came, but he never went. We lived a haunting in a realm that was too personal.

What is interesting about my first book on Norman is the fact it was an archetypal time. I had never chronicled a haunting in real time. He was ours. We had the home-field advantage. Every time something related to Norman would occur, I would document it.

Needless to say, this preface does not even scratch the surface of our experiences with the haunted doll. There is so much more to learn about the haunting we survived. We felt somewhat at ease with the activity remaining content and quiet for so long after locking him away. We believed our problem had been solved.

In 2018, I published an entire book revolving around Norman, the doll haunting our house. The book is titled *Norman: The Doll That Needed to Be Locked Away.* Through that book, you will read firsthand my story in its entirety, and it will help you better understand why we are where we are today.

Introduction

We have all heard that cliché phrase about being in the wrong place at the improper time. Many times, it is mentioned in passing with little to no substance behind it. But other times, like in my life, that expression nearly acted as a credo for my family.

For thirty-one years now, since my first paranormal experience in 1987, I have lived in the life beyond. For thirty-one years, I have seen a dimension reality shows fraudulently sell and nonbelievers mock. For thirty-one years, I have seen a life beyond our tweets, soccer practice for the kids, fake news, viral videos, and who is wearing what at the Oscars.

Our lives seem simple, and they are. Regardless, we tend to only care about life when illness falls upon us. We tend to only care about life when standing somberly at a funeral. Billions of people every day speak of faith. They speak of that yellow brick road that awaits them when the lights go out in their city.

But how many seek it out every day? How many people in this world actually realize that, yes, they are right? There is something after all of this. Can I call it heaven? Can I call it hell?

I can't. However, what those places represent is all up for interpretation. I have seen evil. I have seen bliss. But magic? I never thought much about it. Magic has always been a whimsical parlor trick fueled by logic and manipulation of the mind. Can people truly control an environment by willing it that way or even requesting an effect from a god without some slight of hand involved?

I have to admit, my life in the field of paranormal research has been filled with a preponderant amount of inquisitive confusion.

When people meet me, they instantly assume I am a very religious man. In reality, I am not. I believe in what I see, and when I tell you I have seen some unfathomable supernatural occurrences, you better believe I mean it.

If you have followed along in my journey, you are well aware how views have changed and how I have adapted to the ever-changing realm of the unknown. For me, I don't want to believe a man or woman can have the power to bring forth something from a spiritual realm. It doesn't matter if their intent is genuine and for good, and it doesn't matter if their intent is for something malicious. I just don't want to believe it. My mind cannot wrap around it. I have yet to see a person stand in front of me and bend a spoon or invoke a spirit or heal a sick loved one. But the Norman case made me question a lot of things, not only within myself, but within paranormal science.

I have been on a journey since 1987. I was viciously attacked by an unseen, strong force. From that day forward, I pursued the reasons for it. Thirty-some years later, I still don't know why. But what I do know is *it* is out there.

Monsters and angels exist. Good and evil exist. And when I say that, I am not referring to the standard definitions. Monsters can be many things, and so can angels for that matter.

However, a vintage doll with a tragic history gave me the opportunity to see a different kind of monster. A monster I would have never thought I'd see. There was a power. A power our stiff, professing scientists have yet to measure. Frankly, it's because they can't. Hell, I can't.

All I can do is tell you what happened, what was filmed and recorded, and leave the rest to the universe. Not everything can be measured. Especially when we are basing measurements on human science. I grow tired of that mentality.

We say, no life could possibly exist on other planets because they lack oxygen and water. That mental attitude is asinine. How can we, with a straight face, base everything off of our own requirements for existence?

Again, not everything can be measured.

Having spent the past few years solely focused on documenting a possessed doll, I've opened my mind even more. But I did not expect an ending. I have always said that true ghost stories have no ending. They always are and always will be. Ghosts never die. Energy does not die. Therefore, there is never truly an end.

We asked for it, and furthermore, we should have anticipated it. Were we accurate or even in the right state of mind—considering those previous events—to decide to keep him?

This case, as bizarre and terrifying as it is, did end. And I still to this day can't even accept that, and I was there. Looking back, it was mindless to consider for one second that any of this could have had a happy ending. I always hoped for one, and maybe, in a way, we did find that for a brief moment in time. Yet it was just an ignorant pipe dream to believe there was such a thing as "happily ever after." That's where I stood when it started again.

That forces me to wish I authored fictional stories instead of true accounts of the paranormal. Then maybe the best of times would be something to find trust and comfort in.

Cognitively content, I thought after publishing the book that preceded this one that a chapter of our lives would be left locked away just like he was. You may rid yourself of an entity or a haunting, and that may become the end of your story. But the spirit carries on forever.

In 2016, we acquired a monster—a doll we would later prove to be haunted beyond any terrifying tale ever told. And we proved it by living directly in the line of fire. That was our choice. That was our foolish belief. Embarrassingly, I say arrogance and selfish curiosity led us both to think we were the ones in total control. When in reality, he was the one pulling the strings.

However, at the time, we felt our decision was compassionate. But truth be told, I just didn't want to part with the one thing we had in our possession, and our masquerade of control, that proved the supernatural existed.

Sure, I have seen a lot. I have documented and published a lot concerning my work in the field. But out of all of those stories and experiences, this one has taken the shape of an exhausting and tantalizing obsession.

At one time, I did want him gone, but that was before I witnessed the unimaginable through him. My friend of misery was no longer my friend of mystery...to a point. How could I want him gone when my job is studying paranormal phenomenon? I could never give up such an opportunity. Not now.

Forget the movies. Forget the campfire stories. I think the critics of my first book on Norman said it best. Many of them set Norman on a pedestal above all of the other haunted dolls that have become household names. Annabelle and Robert, the two haunted dolls I mentioned in the preface, come to mind. Although I can't account for their haunted validity, I also can't report on the fact they are not. I haven't been granted that opportunity.

But the critics and television made Norman a household name. On one hand, I am extremely blessed and grateful for that. On the other hand, why did it have to be my household? To think that our doll made readers forget about the others that scared film audiences for years was more than overwhelming and flattering. But at what price?

The toll this experience has taken on our family is nearly immeasurable. Norman has changed our lives forever. Unseeing it is impossible.

Friends, it is not effortless to openly expose monstrous events such as these. There are reputation, credibility, and just plain sanity at stake. We have put Norman out there to act as a learning tool for others, no matter the outcome for us both socially and professionally. Now more than ever, he is more of a being than a plastic toy.

There has been a very common and repetitive question in reviews of the first Norman book and in emails and comments on social media. Why would we keep such a dangerous entity in our home? Some people ask that question in a very accusative manner while others ask it with sincere intentions. Why keep our family purposely in danger? To some, it may sound like we are foolish to do so. To others, you get it. We are a family of paranormal investigators and researchers. I am a phenomenologist. We have accepted this responsibility.

One way or another, somebody is going to accept the responsibility and repercussions of owning Norman. So I answer that question with a question. "Why not us?" There isn't anybody more qualified than two people who have lived years studying and experiencing supernatural processes.

You may have bought this book because you saw Norman on television or on the internet. What you saw on Travel Channel's *A Haunting* is only about 25 percent of the story. There is so much more to learn about.

You may have grabbed this book for one reason or another without any prior knowledge of me or its predecessor. More will be revealed later on concerning previous events, so don't worry about being out of the loop. A lot of previously released footage is also available on social media, so take a look at that. This book is a collection of my notes written out and streamlined to share and continue the saga.

For over twenty years now, I have documented alleged hauntings. In my previous works, each chapter was a story, an experience, and my thoughts concerning a particular case. But in those situations, I was able to walk away from them, and the experiences were written after the fact.

Norman was different. He became his own story, and one we had control of telling. So every day a new entry was added to our journal concerning the living dead doll.

My name is Stephen Lancaster. My involvement in the field of paranormal research spans over two decades. I have worked over one thousand cases in that time and can count on two hands twice over those that truly left me dumbfounded.

I began serious research on the phenomenon known as "troubled objects" three years ago with the main point of focus being Norman the haunted doll. My story, our story, continues.

As I write this, it is July 26, 2019. It was three years ago to the day when we first started to experience strange and unexplainable activity in our home. I took a look back on social media to see what I was saying then.

In a 2016 post dated for today, I said,

> Activity at our house has been on the rise ever since we started collecting haunted objects.
>
> There has always been activity here of some sort over the years and there are at least a dozen witnesses to it. But considering what we do when it comes to research, I always dismissed it as spiritual energy returning home with us.
>
> However it appears to be escalating a lot recently. There has been a lot of emotional turmoil

in the house for the past week (everything is fine, not that kind of emotional) and that may be feeding whatever is here.

We have a surveillance system up in the house. This morning, we caught a wooden totem fly across the bedroom at my back while I was working at the desk and a transparent anomaly appears to the right of the camera prior to the throw. Very interesting stuff.

[We are on] high alert today.

I believe tonight we might do a full on investigation and fire up everything.[1]

As you can probably tell, we never suspected Norman at first. Three years ago today, the Norman saga started to take shape. This post was shortly after we acquired the doll, yet at the time, no fingers were pointing toward him.

Curious events were starting to take place in our house, slowly escalating to what you now know as the phenomenon Norman the doll. But that was then. What do I do now?

The investigative and research part of me wanted to keep going. I wanted to witness just how far this would go. In the world of paranormal research, events and experiences

1. Stephen Lancaster, "Activity at our house has been on the rise ever since we started collecting haunted objects," Facebook, July 26, 2016, https://www.facebook.com/wraithwrite/posts/1580550655578507.

such as these are monumental, and let's face reality here: they are extremely rare.

I mean, after all, this is why I, or we, or maybe even you do it, right? The endless nights. The countless batteries. The cup after cup of coffee. We all have our reasons. Maybe it is scientific discovery. Maybe the motive stems from a personal supernatural experience. Maybe it is simply the selflessness behind using one's years of experience to help others with their own paranormal issues. At this point in my life, and my many years in the field, mine is all three.

Whatever the case, history was being made. And not just any history—an extraordinary one. This was not a bizarre occurrence that could be swept under the rug by our government. This was not a fictitious staged event by a network producer to boost the ratings of a ghost hunting television show. This was historical, concrete, genuine, and factual.

With that being said, this became quite the conundrum when one is an often-sought-out, seasoned paranormal researcher who was in total control of what's real and what's not. Here I was with my own personal case, and I couldn't really explain it. Damned if I did. Damned if I didn't. But damned if I wouldn't. So we continued on with our hell house, our box of mystery, and our doll that was nor toy nor man for the benefit and interest of discovery, and for the hopes of uncovering how and why.

We continued raising hell. We kept researching him, and this is what happened … so far.

1

Dire Eve

Christmas Eve to most people is a time of happiness, family, and celebration. For me, the holiday now represents fear, anxiety, death, and destruction. But it wasn't always like that.

As a child, like most, I looked forward to Christmas: the lights, the presents, the laughs, and the family gathering together. As I grew older, that excitement was still there. The only thing that changed was the direction of my joyfulness.

As a young father, I was blissful with the anticipation of seeing my daughter's face light up Christmas morning. As a grandfather, my emotional joy is directed toward my grandchildren.

Following our first Christmas with Norman and the horrible experiences, the paranormal enthusiast in me took over and the holiday became something I would rather skip.

You know that old idiomatic expression, "The right place at the right time"? That could not be more fitting to define my position on Christmas Eve 2018. If I had not been suffering from yet another sleepless night, we might not even be alive.

It had been nearly two years, and for the most part, the house had been quiet and untroubled as far as the supernatural was concerned. For almost two years, he sat content. Ever since we locked Norman away in his room, the activity originating from him just went away throughout the rest of our house.

Occasionally, we would hear small, subtle sounds coming from his room. Once in a while, we would hear the television inside come off and on. There were times we would even hear Norman talking to himself. We could never make out what was being said after we put an ear to the door. The voices always came across muffled and from a distance. But the activity that did occur never left Norman's room. So quite often we would forget he was even in the house.

Unfortunately, the surveillance system monitoring our home suffered from an electrical surge a few years ago. Each year, North Carolina suffers from torrential storm after storm. It is nothing in the middle of the summer to get hit with tornadoes or hail.

One storm in late winter short-circuited the system. If Norman had been active at the time, I would have certainly blamed him for destroying the surveillance system. I am sure he knows what we had with all of the previous video footage. He is an intelligent entity, so destroying the one thing that constantly caught him in the act made sense. But I can't honestly say it was him that fried the system.

Of course, with Norman lying dormant for so long, the surveillance kind of lost its importance. This was the same surveillance system we installed shortly after welcoming Norman into our lives. In the past, the surveillance moni-toring device would occasionally remind me of the heinous entity locked behind closed doors when I would peek at it. The monitor sat right in our bedroom, which was a huge convenience. Without a doubt, we definitely noticed once we were without it. I did not realize how much we counted on it before.

Our then-neighbors were very sketchy, always commit-ting something unlawful. It was nothing for us to receive an unwanted guest pounding on our front door in the mid-dle of the night. Typically, it was somebody looking for our neighbor, and they were at the wrong house.

We bought a surveillance system to monitor our prop-erty, and it ultimately served a dual purpose. It was placed there initially to protect us from the shady actions of our neighbor and then to help us prove Norman was the source of paranormal activity in our home.

The surveillance served its purpose. We captured more than enough visual evidence to prove our antique shop acquisition was authentically haunted. The footage we captured made headlines, captivated the paranormal community, and was showcased on national television. And of course, our first year with him was chronicled in a nonfiction book.

Norman enjoying his own room

Now, routine checks on his room were mandatory in our home. Norman was always just sitting in his chair staring at the television as if he was watching something nobody else could see. We thought the problem had been solved.

We felt our solution of placing him in his room stopped the haunting of our house.

Unfortunately, Norman became restless.

We knew that Christmastime was always a trigger for the strange activity, but all of the other times never seemed to have a rhyme or reason to them. I guess after a few years of being seated in solitary confinement, he had plenty of time to devise his escape. Admittedly, his plan worked. Flawlessly.

Christmas for my family changed starting with Norman's arrival in 2016. The festive holiday just hasn't been the same. For those three years, there was always some level of paranoia. We all walked on pins and needles with Norman around, knowing that Christmas, for whatever reason, rubbed him the wrong way.

Fifty-seven years ago, Norman killed on Christmas Eve. A young mother, as well as her dog, perished in a fire probably initiated by him back in the 1960s. His death toll rose after we acquired him. He killed again.

He was now up to one human being, a dog, and a kitten. Those are the ones we know of, and we have considered other deaths closely related. Norman attempted to kill me but failed. At least, that is what I believe. Maybe he was just attempting to scare me away when I had my heart attack. Regardless, I survived. I stayed.

My granddaughter and grandson, Lyndsay and Liam, haven't been back to the house since the activity with

Norman hit its apex. Liam being paralyzed and frozen in trances, and watching Norman move his head on surveillance with my grandchildren in the room, was enough to warrant no more visits.

My stepdaughter Hannah, who was living with her older brother, was hesitant to move back in, but eventually she did after some reassurance that Norman was finally at peace. I guess her hesitation was to be expected considering Norman's room was right beside hers.

But here we were again on Christmas Eve: paranoid, full of anxiety, and preparing for another sleepless night. Christina and I went to bed shortly after ten in the evening. Hannah went to bed before us at around eight.

Our bedroom remained unchanged. Everything was pretty much in the same spot it was three years ago, including our defunct surveillance system and monitor for the unit. I refused to order a new system. For months I talked and talked about trying to repair it. I am good with electrical components, repair, and building my own mad scientist inventions. I was determined to eventually fix the old one. Yet there I was, months later, and it still sat there collecting dust. I just never got around to it.

In the past, I had a direct line of sight to the monitor, which displayed the eight cameras wired throughout the house. The camera setup was good fortune and condemning at the same time. On one hand, when something strange happened, it was nice to be able to go back and review exactly what had transpired. On the other hand, I found myself constantly watching it when trying to fall asleep. It was like a live glimpse into my reality. I could view my entire house, inside and out, in real time. Every little creak or crack would cause me to open my eyes and just stare at the monitor, anxiously waiting for something, anything, to happen. It was almost as if I expected it.

Of course, one camera was firmly in place watching over Norman's room. But nothing ever changed on that particular screen. Even when we would hear the television on in his room, the surveillance never showed it. The television wasn't in the camera's frame, but one would think the lighting would change. It never did, however.

You know that old phrase, "I'd rather have it and not need it than need it and not have it"? I completely understand that now. I had told myself that with the surveillance being down, I could be more diligent with my observations and studies of Norman. I would have to be ready at any moment to document with my own cameras and equipment. There was not a reason to have the surveillance system up and running again until that point. Until that vengeful night.

No sugarplums danced in my head that night, that's for sure. Instead, it was visions of Norman creeping around being his mischievous self. I tossed and turned with images of Norman unwaveringly planted in my head. I tried to convince myself that the likelihood of anything extreme happening again after all this time was slim to none. But as history has taught me, ghosts never die and the activity happening again was entirely possible. So I worried.

I mean, how can the aforesaid happen to the same guy twice? This wasn't a *Die Hard* movie. I would later eat those words.

As predicted, I did not sleep. I found myself either staring at the ceiling or agaze at the blank surveillance monitor simply out of habit. I don't know what I was waiting for. It was like I expected it to just turn on, monitoring the whole house again.

Eleven thirty came so fast, it was as if time had forgotten about the past hour and a half.

What saved us that frightful night was my stomach. I was hungry. I crawled out of bed and headed directly for the kitchen to grab something to eat. At first, I thought I was half asleep and half awake, sleepwalking, or both. It appeared as if I was caught in the middle of a dream and reality. Unfortunately, I was definitely awake. Unluckily, it was every bit of real.

On the way back to our bedroom, I saw bright flashes of light coming from underneath Norman's door. I immediately snapped out of the groggy trance. His door was adjacent to the living room and right next to Hannah's bedroom.

The living room was like an aphotic zone. It was so dark, I found myself tripping over dog toys during the mad dash to Norman's room. Upon arrival, I could see light dancing from underneath the door.

Not truly knowing what the hell was going on, I immediately threw myself onto the ground to peer underneath it. What I saw caused me to say, "Holy shit," out loud. I saw Norman sitting in his rocking chair and the carpet underneath him on fire!

My stomach sank knowing that beyond that barrier, a fire was slowly beginning to eat away our home. I was in such a panic, I rushed back to our bedroom, screaming at Christina to wake up while I grabbed my keys. She was confused and startled, and I did not have any time to explain to her the severity of the situation.

During all of the commotion, Hannah woke up and came running out of her room just in time to see me struggling with the set of keys in an attempt to find the one that unlocked Norman's door. All I could think about was how Norman's room was right next to Hannah's, and the house was literally catching fire.

I finally found the correct key and raced back to his threshold. There was no other alternative. I had to open the damned door.

By the time I was able to enter the room, Norman had begun burning himself. The right side of him was starting to catch fire. Flames randomly kissed his plastic skin and hair.

Without a second thought, I grabbed Norman and started beating his head on the burning and smoking carpet to put him and the floor out.

Thankfully, I succeeded.

I turned around to see Christina and Hannah standing in the doorway with confused looks on their faces. I told them I had no clue how this happened.

There was nothing electrical or mechanical around Norman and his rocking chair. In other words, there was not anything of note that could have caused a fire accidentally, purposefully, or logically. What occurred was paranormal by every account.

I explained that I was awake and saw something out of place as I walked from the kitchen.

If I would not have been awake, our house, with us in it, would have burned to the ground. Norman included.

Hannah started crying and shaking while Christina held her as they stood in the doorway. I remained still for a moment as I held Norman by his hand. My arm was to the side as he swung in a subtle fashion, dangling from my hand.

As I stood there in a hypnotic state, all I could smell was burnt carpet and plastic. Christina was quick to point out that I was standing and holding Norman exactly like the little girl did in 1968. While she was standing barefoot in the snow watching her house burn on Christmas Eve, I was standing in a child's room after preventing ours from meeting the same fate. I thought at that moment everything had come full circle. I now shared a similar experience with the little girl that originally owned Norman over fifty years ago.

I glanced down at Norman, and all I could focus on was that sinister little smile and hypnotic gaze. Within moments, I broke free of my enchantment and walked out with Norman in tow, passing Christina and Hannah as I headed back to our bedroom.

I sat on the bed with the doll beside me, just shaking my head in disbelief. Norman sat up next to me as if a father and son were about to have an important life lesson talk. Only I had nothing to say to him. I was still in shock.

He was back. He was back with a vengeance.

I looked at the clock, and it was just past midnight. Christmas day was officially here, and Norman had the hottest gift of the year to give us. The fire in his room would act as a prelude for the events to come. My entire family was already on edge, and rightfully so. None of us could have predicted what was about to happen next.

2

Roasting on an Open Fire

Christina and Hannah joined me in the bedroom.

I could read the curiosity on my wife's face. Without saying a word, her bold and confused expression asked me how Norman's room caught fire. I just looked at her and said, "I have no idea. But thank the powers that be I was in the right place at the right time."

Hannah had calmed down enough to talk, and now all four of us were sitting on the bed. One dysfunctional family once again haunted by the past.

Norman's appearance had altered drastically. No longer did he have the cute, yet sinister exterior. This event changed his entire aura and added a daunting, haunting visual aspect that not only captivated you, but shook your very soul to the absolute core. I could even smell the residue from the burns, and I wasn't even close enough for that.

You know when a pungent smell just lodges itself within the inner walls of your nose and no matter where you go or what you do you can smell it?

His wounds momentarily became the incense of our bedroom. It was a mordacious odor. I felt like I was breathing poison with every breath I took. As I am writing this, I can still relive that smell. It wasn't like wood burning or charcoal or that wonderful smell of a home-cooked meal. It was dark, saturating, and viciously poisoning. The odor felt like a blanket of sorrow was covering us.

No matter what, it always seemed that anything surrounding Norman, even on the smallest of levels, grew into something much larger and encompassing. Even as an unscathed, brand new toy, Matty Mattel's face appeared sly, mischievous, and contemplating shenanigans, without the need for being possessed by a threatening being. At least, that's how he appeared to me. His already in place *naughty* look became more fitting once I learned he was being controlled by an immoral spirit.

He was now 100 percent menacing looking. The fire brought a life to his exterior that wasn't there prior. It was still Norman on the surface, but the accents of burns gave him the appearance of one hundred faces in one. Depending on which way or what angle you looked at him, Norman seemed to have a different persona thanks to the repercussions of the fire and the new shadows that now laced his face.

Norman before the fire

Now his look was more fitting and what one would expect something harboring a dark evil to appear as. He no longer looked like an innocent toy. The burns only effected his face, which is still a conundrum to this day. Logically, considering the fire was underneath him, his bottom half should have burned first. Instead, it did not burn at all.

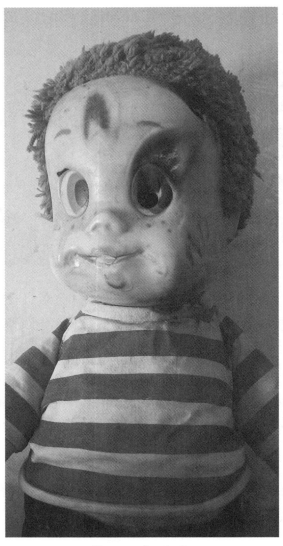

Norman after the fire

The impish little doll was now forever scarred. There was no way to turn back time. There was no way to replace him. He grew into that. That was the Norman we lived with now.

One of the changes in his appearance I noticed immediately was what appeared to be a perpetual tear pouring down his face. Mattel's original, mass-marketed doll from 1962 was not designed to cry or even look like it had been crying.

The tear

The logical side of me attributed that to the fire. The paranormal side of me blamed something far worse. Was there an innocent little boy trapped inside with a malevolent entity or enraged spirit? It just wasn't adding up. All of my data was pointing to something evil. At the same time, it was also pointing to the spirit of a stillborn child. One of two things was happening here. Either the child was lashing out at a world he could never have or he was trapped with a sinister being. That was something to definitely consider. There was still a chance the child had nothing to do with the doll at all. There are no rules to this game. Who is to say that multiple spirits can't haunt the same object?

We knew whatever was inside of Norman was evil. At one time, we believed a child spirit to be trapped inside of Norman. In other instances we believed it to be an older man. Although, I felt the spirit was that of the unborn boy, and he aged mentally by observation. In the end, it was nearly impossible to prove which of our theories was true.

Whatever the entity was, it could appear and act like anything, and that was a very scary realization to digest. But the tear was dumbfounding. It meant something. I had seen a lot of questionable things during my time in the field of paranormal research, and biological functioning was never one of them. How does a tear appear opposite the side that was burned? How does a tear even appear at all? There was not any damage to stage right of his face; in the pictures, it is on the left for you readers. Not a single burn mark or even an inkling of melting. The tear was on top of the cheek and layered over the plastic. That was perplexing to say the least.

At first, I thought maybe Norman was trying to leave this world by destroying his shell. His toy body could have been viewed as a coffin, I suppose. Maybe he was trying to finally move on. I wanted to believe that he wasn't trying to kill us, but I think that was more or less me attempting to reassure myself, Christina, and Hannah.

With Norman being who he was, it was very difficult to determine genuine emotions from him. It could be a ploy for all we knew. It could all be just another tactic to lure us in and put our guard to rest. When dealing with something evil, you never truly know when to believe what you are seeing. Appearances can often be deceiving, and oftentimes deceit is the true nature of their origins.

However, my thoughts would always land right back on the same idea. He was trying to kill us. That has seemed to be his stratagem from the beginning. It certainly was with me. Could he have been angry for being locked away instead of finding himself relieved and at a level of serenity?

I concluded that he was out for revenge. There were many things he could have chosen to do to garner attention. But he went straight for one of the most dangerous methods. He was either counting on me to be awake, knew I was already awake, or fully intended to just burn it all to the ground.

Seeing what Norman could do in the past and knowing the terror my family lived through, it was hard to think otherwise. I think he was trying to take us all down. We knew his secret.

Before any of us could attempt to rest, I needed to do something with Norman. Christina finally talked Hannah into going back to bed, but first she wanted reassurance that Norman would not be returning to the room next to hers. She also made it clear that she wanted him locked up and more confined. She knew we had attempted to rid ourselves of him before and that had failed. So for Hannah, locking him up and placing him as far from her as possible was the only way she was going to negotiate.

He was Christina's and my responsibility now more than ever. He needed to stay where we could see him. With no surveillance, we had no choice but to keep him in our bedroom. The bedroom also doubled as my study, so ninety percent of the time, one of us was in there.

Plus, I had easy access to all of my cameras and equipment. If things were to head south again, I could document on a whim.

I had placed him in what I call a "glass coffin," a glass exhibit case typically used for displaying dolls, figures, collectibles, or anything you wish to keep protected. In this particular situation, the case was to protect us, or at least I had hoped.

At least in the case it would be harder to burn anything. Carpet is one thing, but a glass case is another.

Norman back in his glass case

Glass can break, however, and I was beginning to think there was no foolproof way of containing him.

I felt like we had taken a step backwards with Norman. He was once again tucked away in our bedroom and right in the middle of our family, just like he was years ago. At this point in the very early hours of the morning, all I could do was stare up at Norman, who once again was king of my research castle.

I was so engulfed with terrible thoughts about Norman, I had not taken the time to even allow myself to be blessed or merry for Christmas. I knew it was Christmas, but it was far from feeling like it. All I could think about was the outstanding possibility that we could have been burned alive in our sleep, in our house, and nobody would have ever truly known why.

Those anonymity-filled events do occur. Heart attacks, tragedy-stricken circumstances such as a fire, and the reality of literally being scared to death happen at the hands of monstrous entities more than you think. I think most people just choose to ignore them.

Terrible thoughts overcame me as I envisioned those things happening. I found it very difficult to snap myself back into reality as I attempted to fall asleep. Every time I closed my eyes, all I could see were Hannah and Christina screaming as they burned, and me, unable to do anything to stop it.

Losing all we have in a fire has been one of my greatest fears, and that almost became a reality. But for Norman, he wasn't going to let me rest in the slightest. He had more than a fireworks show to put on.

3

Burn

I rolled over to look at Christina, and she was already staring back at me. It was evident what was on both of our minds. Norman.

Christina and I did not say a word to one another. We just stared. I guess you could say that was a traumatic enough event to put us both in a state of shock and disbelief. I know I was questioning everything at that point.

Truth be known, I really could not sleep because deep down I was waiting for the doll to strike again. Whatever the intent behind catching his room on fire, it was interrupted by me. Maybe that was what he wanted. Maybe he forced my hand so he would once again be brought back out. After a few years of living with Norman, I grew to expect more and more if he started his haunting cycle again. I was not wrong in that belief. Once he started haunting our house in

2016, he did not halt until we stopped him by placing him under lock and key in his own room. Why should this time be any different?

I rolled over to face away from Christina and check the clock. It was now two in the morning. To me, it felt like it should have been eight in the morning. Watching the walls and the ceiling and just staring off felt like observing and waiting for a pot of water to boil. One minute felt like ten minutes.

But it was within that moment that I noticed light bouncing off of our bedroom walls and ceiling. The light sporadically and unpredictably shot rays across our room as if outside a party was taking place.

The lights flickered and flashed like a strobe light or sunlight hitting a disco ball. Red and orange and spellbinding. I knew there was nothing firing light off in our bedroom.

I got up from the bed and walked out into the living room, but to my chagrin, no source of the light could be found. The living room was as dark as I left it. I turned to walk back into the bedroom, and that's when I noticed where all of the light was coming from.

There are windows on both sides of our bed, and through those windows, I could see the colors of cherry red and citrus fruit pulsating. As I stood in our bedroom doorway, Christina asked me what was wrong. I told her something must be going on outside. This prompted us both to move one of the curtains and have a look.

It was lurid, to say the least. I literally threw my hand across my gaping mouth. Our barn was completely engulfed in flames!

As quickly as we could, Christina and I threw some decent clothes and shoes on, grabbed our cell phones, screamed for Hannah, and we all ran outside to the burning building out back. The barn was only about thirty feet from our house.

The building went up so fast. Quicker than anything I have ever witnessed burn. I stood there in a trance watching the fire dance and flicker. My mind tried to make sense of it all as I saw face after face appear in the flames. Logic convinced me they weren't really faces. Prior experience convinced me they might have been. But the fire appeared to be alive as it digested the flesh of the structure. It was like watching passing souls aim for the sky. Yet there was not any bright, white light at the end of the tunnel. The sky was black and gray and very unwelcoming. I had my hand over my mouth the whole time.

I stood there entranced with every flame that reached for the sky. Each flame held a phantom-like presence. They were like wispy ghosts coming from hell. In many ways, they were coming from hell. Just not the devil's hell. It was our hell.

The three of us stood there in silence. My heart was pounding against my chest as I envisioned our own house burning to the ground. That could have been our house just hours ago.

There was no saving it. We didn't even bother calling the fire department. Once we ruled out the fire touching our house, we just allowed history to take place. Within minutes, only the bones of the building remained burning. The remaining beams reminded me of some sort of tribal altar used for religious rituals.

The barn burning

With the fire reaching for the heavens, it was quite the sight to observe. What were the chances of two fires, involving the same people, in the same night?

More images of Norman flooded my mind, like a freight train racing through my thoughts with that damned doll as the engineer. Norman wanted a fire. Norman wanted to destroy something, and ultimately, he did.

Steve and his wife, our new neighbors since October of 2018, quickly joined us out by the burning barn. Their dogs had awakened them by barking at us and the commotion outside. It was not long before they took a peek out their window, noticed the fire outside, and saw us. Our new neighbors were certainly receiving their first hazing from the paranormal world. That's what happens when you move next to us.

The fire and disruption woke up nearly everybody on our street, and it wasn't long before we had an audience.

Our dogs, left in the house, were barking like rabid animals. Dogs barking, people gasping, whispers among the crowd, people crying, and of course, the crackling of old wood burning to the ground.

Big Steve (the nickname we gave him to halt confusion with two Stephens in the neighborhood) used his tractor to take control of the fire by pushing the crumbling structure into a smaller pile. The barn was used as a shelter for our horse, Molly. All that was in it was hay and a few farming tools. Luckily for us, all that surrounded the barn was the green grass that acted as a pasture for Molly. Nothing else was going to burn. Well, nothing else was near enough to catch fire because of the farm building burning.

While our neighbor was busy wrangling the fire, one of our other neighbors asked if we had seen her dog Brownie.

She told us that her dog had been let outside on Christmas Eve but never returned. Within moments, all of us started scouring the neighborhood in search of Brownie.

Sadly, after about twenty minutes of searching, he was discovered dead in a ditch a few houses down the street. That moment was very hard to digest. I am a huge animal lover, so I can't describe enough the difficulty of that situation. Losing a dog, to me, is like losing a child, and I could only imagine what my neighbor was feeling at that moment. I could only assume that Brownie must have been sleeping in our barn when the fire started. That was the last place he was seen. The fire must have forced him out. It was extremely difficult to even look, and I will leave what happened to him up to your own interpretation.

I cannot say whether or not Norman had anything to do with it with certainty. All I can do is consider what Norman has been to blame for in the past. We had proven he was responsible for horrifying and tragic events before. You can only call it coincidence so many times. He started a fire in our house and actually burned down our entire barn. I had no choice but to believe that whether I could prove it or not.

After everybody calmed down, our neighbors all returned home. Big Steve had the fire comfortably under control, so we decided to go back into the house.

If what had transpired so far wasn't personal enough, the activity and attacks escalated to a more vindictive level. I am literally gritting my teeth in anger as I relive this moment.

If you know me personally, you know I love my dogs. You know my number one guy is my dog Tank. I would take a bullet for him. He is without a doubt my best friend. He is a Bernese Mountain Dog and Labrador mix. Loyal, tough, and loving as can be.

Tank has been trained to investigate and often accompanies us on paranormal investigations. He has his own rig with supplies and an infrared head cam when we take him out. After all, animals can see things we cannot. This is the same dog, years ago, I watched walk backward out of the kitchen because Norman was in there. This is the same dog, years ago, who captured Norman on video in mid-air through his head cam.

Tank: the alpha

Before I continue, it should be noted that Tank is a big boy. He's a lovable dog, but his size demands respect, and often he can come off quite daunting. We currently have six dogs in our house, and Tank is firmly the alpha. There isn't a single dog we have that could beat him in a fight, nor would they even try.

TANK CAM 10/2016

Norman jumping from the table

I am telling you all of this because what we walked into upon returning to the house still has me shaking my head in disbelief.

We walked into the house in hopes of placing the events of that evening and early morning to rest, along with ourselves. Instead, we walked into our living room to find Tank panting and moaning and severely wounded from an attack. You read that right.

He was alive and is still alive today, but something attacked him, and it wasn't an animal. He had wounds around his neck and snout. They were very precise and clean scratches. They reminded me of tiny, intricate medical incisions one would see a professional surgeon perform during a surgery

Something tried to tear him to shreds. Blood was all over the floor and all over him, but he was the only one bleeding. I quickly grabbed a towel from the laundry room and wrapped it around Tank. I cleaned him up the best I could and sat with him until his anxiety ceased. After he calmed down, we tended to his wounds. Christina being a retired nurse certainly helped in that department.

Hannah couldn't handle the situation, and I don't blame her. The night had been one extreme after the other. That was a lot for an eighteen-year-old to take in, even considering she was quite used to this lifestyle from living with us. Surprisingly, she pushed through and did not ask us to leave.

Christina examined our other dogs fully, expecting to find one in a similar state as Tank. But to her amazement and mine, there was not a scratch on any of the others. There was not an inkling of blood or signs of fighting on any of them. Now, they all acted timidly. Our smallest dog, Buddy, was nearly crawling on the floor when he walked. He was obviously wary of something.

We knew people were going to ask what had happened to Tank, so we just told them he was in a fight with another dog outside. I mean, how do you tell the mail carrier that a smiling toy from the sixties attacked our dog? Something had taken place in our house while we were outside. Something sinister and downright evil. But as far as the public was concerned, that remained unsaid.

In my mind, and thinking strategically, it makes sense to go after the alphas. You declare dominance that way. Norman went after me in the past, and now he had gone after our strongest dog. With that in mind, I believed that Norman was staking a claim to dominance and telling us that we had no power that would intimidate him. He was a spirit and with that came attributes we did not have. I think he believed we were impotent to the situation.

After everything calmed down, Christina and I made our way back to the bedroom. Like before, Christina and I were on our backs in bed, attempting to find a glimmer of rest, and staring at the ceiling with Norman overseeing the room. All I could smell was fire. Our clothes were blanketed in that smell, and it didn't help that Norman's room was on fire earlier.

This was beyond alarming. This was on the far side of reasoning. This was well past my comfort zone. In just a few hours, Norman managed to completely outshine nearly everything he had ever done in the past as far as my family was concerned. In a short time, Norman managed to alter

his appearance in an attempt to burn down our house, succeeded in destroying our barn, and succeeded in putting
us back on high alert. I could only point to Norman when
it came to the Tank situation. So whatever transpired was
paranormal.

Fear, anxiety, death, and destruction. Why would we
keep this doll? To put it simply, for the sake of extraordinary paranormal research. It is hard to rid yourself of something that proves everything you have tried to validate for
years when it comes to the supernatural.

But even that desire and that passion have their limitations, and I would eventually come to a decision that would
involve ridding ourselves of him. But for now, we continued
to watch. What could have possibly been next? Just how
intelligent was this entity?

4

It Was in the Stars

It was now five thirty in the morning on a not-so-very Merry Christmas. No matter where you stood in our bedroom, Norman always seemed to be looking right at you. As I stared at him, I wondered if he (or it) was even still inside the plastic shell.

I hated to consider that the evil inside had been officially and permanently released when that insane light show occurred. Was it now in our home? Would we be seeing the creature that was briefly captured in an image during Hurricane Matthew two years ago? That was a terrifying thought considering what he accomplished already from *inside* the doll.

I also considered that maybe he was being misread. I have seen children and even adults act bizarre, out of character, and even violent when something deep inside is diluting their mental health. We've all been there. We've all said and done things as a result of being caught up in the moment. Part of me really wanted to believe that Norman was doing what he could. The world and our universe present us with signs every day. Some of us choose to ignore them. Some of us fail to see them altogether. And some of us see things for what they are. I had to ask myself if Norman's signs were misinterpreted. Call it denial. I wanted to believe he truly did not mean harm by his actions. But that was a fool's wishful thinking. I will never forget my cat, Little F, and what happened to him. That was a sight that will forever stay scarred in my psyche.

I remained awake until finally overcoming insomnia around six in the morning, not fully knowing what to expect other than the absence of every person we cared about. That was a lesson learned from the torment of Norman years prior on that day.

We made the difficult decision to keep family absent, which is not traditional for us. That came as quite the shock to our loved ones, who were fully expecting the annual gathering. Our Christmas always came with the expectation of laughter, music, special time with family, sharing gifts, and getting a fatter belly throughout the day.

Needless to say, Christmas morning failed to deliver such things. In fact, it brought forth the epitome of irony. I could not have been asleep for more than fifteen minutes when I awoke to the sound of distant giggling.

The laughter was coming from inside the bedroom, and that was the odd part about the timbre. The titter sounded like it was coming from a distance. I rolled over and sat up on the bed in an attempt to figure out the laughing. The maniacal sound was definitely close to my ear, yet it sounded like it was bellowing up from a deep hole within the bedroom.

Norman was the only thing I knew of that had a deep hole full of gnarly happenings. Christina was finally asleep, so I did not bother to wake her.

The room was semi-lit from the windows as the sun was slowly welcoming the day. There was also a bit of light coming from my computer monitor. Needless to say, I could see fairly well in the room. Nothing seemed out of order, and I started to believe that maybe I had dreamed the whole thing.

That's when I suddenly heard what could only be described as plastic tapping plastic. I was confused. The sound was faint, and I could clearly see that nothing in our bedroom was the cause. That's when my attention was directed to the closet door. Whatever was making that sound was coming from behind the closed door. I walked over to place my ear on the door to hear a little better.

Now I could hear the plastic sound even clearer. It sounded like dozens of toy drumsticks tapping together. I cautiously opened the closet door to see the empty clothes hangers swinging on the rack back and forth. I was shocked, considering there was nothing in the closet to make them move. There also wasn't any air current behind that closed door.

In fact, when I first opened the door, I felt a significant difference in temperature between our bedroom and the closet. The closet was burning up. And as a reminder, this was December. We run floor heaters throughout the winter, and never has one been placed in the closest. There was no explanation as to why the closet was at least twenty degrees warmer.

I continued to stare at the swinging hangers when the whole narrative decided to change to something more symbolic. The hangers slowed down lazily right in front of my eyes and began swinging tardily from side to side as opposed to back and forth.

Their momentum died to nearly a snail's pace before turning and forming two individual pentagrams. My shoulders dropped; I gasped and breathed out a long, heavy sigh. Imagine laying two clothes hangers on the floor with one perfectly aligned on top of the other. Picture the top one turning until the two appear to become a star. Only these were not on the floor, and the shadows cast against the wall looked just like pentagrams.

I literally gritted my teeth and said aloud, "Norman," in a very sharp fashion.

Standing there, I immediately started thinking about the history of Christmas and Neopagan faiths.

That beautiful and iconic glowing star atop our decorated Christmas tree lost it's luster the moment more curious and disturbing stars began to present themselves within our home. There, in turn, was the irony. Pentagrams.

Old history studies started flowing through my head, full of ideas as to which meaning was intended by this. The birthday of Jesus Christ, as most of you know, is celebrated on Christmas Day. Historically speaking, the infamous pentagram image was used to symbolize the five sacrificial wounds of Jesus.

People don't actually realize how many Pagan traditions they take part in when ripping open presents on Christmas. Early church leaders melded together the nativity celebration of Jesus Christ with already existing midwinter Pagan festivals.

A pentagram is sometimes referred to as a "pentalpha," "pentangle," or "star pentagon." All are drawn with five straight strokes in the shape of a five-pointed star. Pentagrams were used religiously in ancient Babylonia and Greece. In modern day, they are used by many Wiccans as a symbol of faith.

Of course, there are many magical associations. Many practitioners of Neopagan faiths wear jewelry that incorporates the popular symbol. It also has associations with Freemasonry. Most likely the most infamous group is the Church of Satan. The inverted pentagram is their copyrighted logo.

English occultist Aleister Crowley used the pentagram in the Thelemic system of magick. He inverted the Pentagram to represent the transition of spirit into physical matter.

Most notable, and most likely the most popular belief about the pentagram in modern day, is that it represents the devil and all things against the Christian God. This is a common misconception. In the past fifty years, the pentagram has been used in horror movies, on album covers and shirts for rock bands, and in an onslaught of books.

All of those examples use it as something evil instead of using it to dispel evil associations. The pentagram is one of the most commonly mislabeled symbols in our history and everyday practice. By the majority, it is commonly used for the greater good and has nothing to do with the negative antics it is so often associated with.

So the answer was in the stars.

I believe that Norman used that image to spark more fear throughout our household. Like many people who are uneducated on its actual use in spiritual practice, I think Norman intended for it to be taken as it is often misconstrued in pop culture.

As I said before, most people view it as symbolizing demons or Satan worship and just downright evil in general. I think Norman thought I would assume his activity to be rooted in evil. He was right. I did at first. But after my thoughts cleared and I remembered the diversity and origin of the symbol, the intended impact of Norman's stunt became watered down.

As if Christina and I weren't convinced enough that a spirit resided in Norman, the unpredictable appearance of pentagrams signed, sealed, and delivered the fact a spirit was, or still is, in a physical form. Those hangers didn't move on their own. Something unseen turned them, and that takes force. Although the spirit possessing him doesn't have mass, it's energy is so great that the doll is capable of interacting and manipulating the environment of the living world with ease. Energy or not, he can touch things.

At this point, knowing what we knew and living what we had, I was up for anything that could bring more answers to the table. And to be honest, I was finding myself for the first time seeking out help on the matter. I was starting to be more open to the idea that maybe there was a demon inside of Norman.

I would further include leading paranormal experts Rosemary Ellen Guiley and Darren Evans in the new re-search. After reviewing every ounce of the Norman case file, they both leaned toward the demonic. They believed the doll to be inhabited by a demonic entity with sinister volition.

I still don't know what I believe in that department, but what we could agree on is the fact that Norman has evil intentions.

But I couldn't let it drag me down. After shaking off the pentagrams, I gave up on the bed and started my day. That consisted of letting all of our dogs outside. I walked back into the house to start preparing their food bowls when I saw him.

There wasn't any prelude or build up or tension. He was just there without warning. I stopped dead in my tracks as I witnessed a full-blown, full-body apparition walk right through the door to Norman's old room.

I literally felt my heart palpitate and skip a few beats. During my amazement, I completely lost focus on what I was doing and dropped the bag of dog food all over the living room floor.

What I saw was an intimidating old man. He was very tall. His head was less than a foot from the ceiling. My mystery apparition was well dressed in a black suit. He did not look like the stereotypical and commercialized "ghost" image. The one second I saw him felt like ten seconds. It was that same feeling you get when you accidentally touch a hot pot.

In 2016, we witnessed the shadow entity during Hurricane Matthew.

Now in 2018, and playing along with my theory that what was inside of Norman was an aged man, I witnessed a completely manifested, unmistakeable apparition with all of the detail in the world.

The entity in the mirror

His image latched onto my brain. I could recall every little detail about him. He looked to be well over fifty years old. This old man wasn't a silhouette or shadow or black mass. He was fully detailed to the point he would almost be considered biological in design. If I had not known better or witnessed him pass through a closed door, I would have easily thought a real, living and breathing person had broken into our home. He was just that convincing.

Was this another version of the dark, black figure, or was what I saw this time his true appearance? Was I finally seeing Norman's ghost? In the paranormal field, it is common knowledge that spirits can manifest differently depending on the environment and available energy sources. Maybe there was enough energy from devices in that area to pull from. Maybe there was enough to show me his true form. It is well known throughout the paranormal community that spirits can and do come in all shapes and sizes. Sometimes we see them as orbs or spheres, and this typically is viewed as an infantile stage. In other cases, we witness a ghost as wispy smoke or even moving shadows in the shape of a person's sihlouette. Finally, if all of the elements are just right through energy and atmosphere, we can view the entity with better clarity and detail as they become a full-bodied apparition.

What is confusing to me is how during hurricane Matthew, where he had an abundance of energy to pull from, Norman only manifested as a black shadowy mass. Whereas, when I saw him as an old man, there wasn't anything outrageous or massively different with the environment. Honestly, I would have expected these experiences to have been reversed where the old man made an appearance during the hurricane instead of the dark figure. All I can say is, all of these thoughts led to more questions. Most importantly: did I just witness his true self?

I could not say. But everything was pointing in that direction.

Chris Beck, one of my trusted research colleagues, is a sketch artist I hire for re-creation purposes. I called upon him to sketch, per my detailed description, the man I saw walking through Norman's door. I think it goes without saying that I wish I had a video of what I saw exactly. But not everything happens the way we want it to.

The paranormal world is so unpredictable, the only real way to ensure everything is covered at any given time is by means of full monitoring surveillance. But that wasn't an option with our system being down. In the end it didn't matter anyway. I knew what I had seen.

In my life, I have seen a handful of full-bodied apparitions across various cases, but this one had a lot more detail. In the past, the figures I had seen during investigations gave you the sense of a being, rather than a full-fledged mock-up of one. Ghosts typically have a transparent quality to them. They appear to look like a person that once was. What I had just seen could have easily fooled anybody. He looked just as real as a person you might see in the supermarket.

The likelihood of this figure being unrelated to Norman was slim to none, especially considering he vanished into the doll's old room. I consider it luck that I even saw him at all, but I am glad I did. It made me wonder just how many times this figure may have been roaming throughout our house in the past and we never knew.

It is hard to say whether or not he wanted me to see him. I chalk it up to good timing. It certainly added another layer to the already bewildering case on the haunted doll. Another piece to the puzzle was added.

Without a photograph to present to you, all I can provide is a sketch of him courtesy of Mr. Beck. Chris hit a chord and nailed his rendition perfectly.

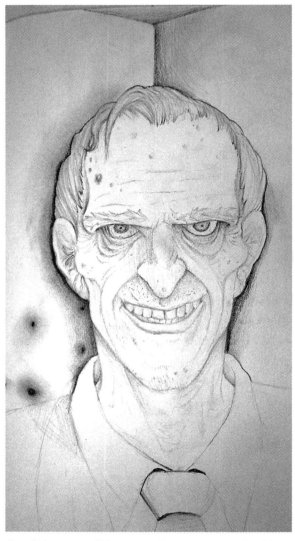

Artist's depiction of Norman as the apparition of the old man

What I saw was no joke. Serious, intense, and hauntingly intimidating. I see this image often when I lie down for bed, wondering and waiting to see him again. But there had to be more. What was causing these manifestations? How could I bring him out on command? Was that even possible?

5

Bound

Back in late December of 2018, I was contacted by a producer via email through my official author page on social media. The funny part about that is the fact it took me forever to even read it. Most emails I receive through that social media outlet consist of readers wanting to discuss my books or my cases, or individuals will contact me wanting an opinion on a photograph or video they believe contains something of paranormal origin.

I receive a lot of correspondence, and I honestly make an attempt each day to address a few. With that being said, it took me about two weeks to get to her email.

Her name was Dawn, and she was very curious about Norman the doll. She even went so far as to say that their company doesn't often seek out something of interest. They typically wait for pitches and ideas to be sent to them.

Her initial email was an invitation to speak on the phone about my book *Norman* and the experiences my family had with him. I acknowledged her request, and she told me she represented a company called New Dominion Pictures. They were extremely interested in filming my story of Norman for their paranormal anthology program, *A Haunting*.

At first, I was skeptical. I always am when it comes to the entertainment industry. I mean, let's face facts, we have all seen what television has done to the paranormal field. And it sure as shit hasn't helped it. But I agreed to at least hear her out.

We set up a phone meeting, and I listened. I was very impressed with Dawn's authenticity and willingness to hear the story as it should be told. I have spoken with nearly one hundred producers over the past twenty years, and none of them ever came close to sounding as genuine as she did. In fact, most of them sound like an overzealous car salesman hoping you are going to become giddy over a chance to be on television. Not this cowboy. I have heard and seen too much bullshit straight from the puppeteers of a lot of these paranormal shows.

Over the years, I have worked with various producers and production companies on paranormal projects for national television. Being behind the scenes on these shows really opened my eyes to the actual reality concerning their intent. Sadly, the intentions of a large portion of them were to manipulate facts and manufacture fraudulent material for entertainment, ratings, and advertising purposes. I learned rather quickly the show was never about the truth.

On numerous occasions, I watched as producers would take multiple lines of dialog from a testimony, cut them up, and move words around to form a sentence that said something completely different from what the person initially intended. Worse yet, I have witnessed producers stage paranormal activity without telling the cast just so they could get a genuine reaction from them. It doesn't get any more fake than that.

Needless to say, Dawn from New Dominion Pictures and *A Haunting* had all of the right things to say. We would be telling the story factually. I agreed to do it with the promise there would be no blowing anything out of proportion, fabricating, or misrepresenting facts.

The show format is a lot different from the stereotypical ghost hunting programs. I mean, let's face it. All of the investigative shows are the same. The only thing that ever changes are the faces in front of the cameras.

With *A Haunting* willing to allow my family and me to tell our story and have it faithfully recreated as it was told through dramatization, I couldn't help but get a little excited. I was being given the opportunity to see my book on Norman come to life.

And I wanted a little help from my friends.

Thanks to my career, I know things, and I know people who know things. With that comes knowing people who are beating the industry by being a part of it.

When I first discovered what Norman could do, and when I began documenting his unbelievable behavior, I turned to research colleagues for validation. After all, this was my haunt, my house, and my bias. This wasn't a case I was working for someone else. This was a case I needed somebody, aside from me and Christina, to work. I sent all of the surveillance footage to trusted colleagues.

Author Shannon Sylvia of Ghost Hunters International; the world-renowned Rosemary Ellen Guiley; and my great friend, my brother, Darren Evans, a demonologist and pioneer of the paranormal field, all watched what I did. They read all of the notes in my case logs. They reviewed every second of footage I had concerning the doll. It was important to me to get Shannon's opinion. She and I worked together in the field, and she is one of the strictest I know when it comes to authenticating or disproving a haunting. It was also vital to garner an opinion from someone outside of the box, and that's why I contacted Rose. She had a generation of knowledge on the occult and haunted objects.

Little did I know that showing my old friend Darren the footage would lead to such extraordinary events. Alongside myself, Christina, and Hannah, Darren and Rosemary were asked to join the production.

A month later, my family and I were packing to head north and film the episode for the show. Darren and Rosemary were boarding a plane to head the same way. But the question was, do I take Norman?

I wouldn't learn until after arriving at New Dominion Pictures that the producers were against the idea. I assumed they would want shots of him and actually use him in the show. As I would later learn, that wasn't the case. They were going to use a "stand in" doll to recreate my story of Norman. I found that kind of funny coming from a crew that produces paranormal television. And without knowing all that prior to our trip, I decided to bring him. Regardless, they did not want that "thing," as they called him, anywhere near them.

I still to this day wonder if we would have ever stumbled upon what else Norman could do if I had not accepted the invitation to appear on *A Haunting*. Considering paranormal research, taking Norman was the best decision I ever made.

Christina, Hannah, and I were Virginia bound. It was Friday, January 25, 2019.

From where we live in North Carolina, the drive would take us a little over three hours. Our check-in time at the hotel in Suffolk, Virginia was at 3 p.m., so we left a little before noon that day. Norman was also bound for Virginia that day. I was bringing him with us.

Excluding the many times I tried to ship him off years ago, this was the first time the three of us had him out of the house, let alone heading out of the state. In the first book about Norman, I explained in great detail the difficulty of taking him from the confines of our house. It was the strangest thing. He would always come back to us. But here we were, heading to Virginia, with a devious haunted doll in tow.

Now, I suffer from post-traumatic stress disorder from a near-fatal car accident that occurred back in 2014. Anybody who personally knows me is well aware of the fact that getting into a vehicle nearly takes an act of Congress. I have written about that experience, too, in a previous book.

But to keep it simple, I flipped a car seven times down a highway on Oak Island. According to officials, I should have been dead. Yet here I am.

That accident, even now, five years later, still haunts me. I still don't drive unless I am placed in an emergency situation that I cannot avoid. With that being said, Christina handles all of the driving. So traveling in a vehicle, even for a short distance, really takes a toll on my anxiety.

A three-hour drive ahead of us was enough to have me already gripping the handle above the passenger side window. Let alone the fact I sit so tense that when I exit a vehicle, I feel like I'm thawing myself out because all of my muscles are so tight.

Then of course, Norman is resting behind me in his old, antique suitcase. Some may laugh, but traveling is my greatest fear. Add Norman to that mix, and my anxiety was on overload.

We were bound for Virginia. Norman was bound in his case. I was bound for a panic attack, and as a family we were bound to a fear-inducing ride.

None of us talked much during the first hour and a half. It is really rare for us to be so silent. People have literally nicknamed me the "mouth from the South," (even though I'm not from the South originally) because I talk at great lengths almost always.

I could, however, feel some tension from Hannah. She would repeatedly bring up the fact that she wasn't happy Norman was in a case on the seat next to her. Every time I looked back at her, she was biting her fingernails in a nervous fashion. That's not something I had ever really seen her do before. At first, I attributed that to simply being nervous about filming for a television show.

I know she was excited about it. For an eighteen-year-old girl to receive an opportunity to be on national television, that had to be pretty thrilling for her. For me, I couldn't have cared less. I like being behind cameras. I was more happy for the fact that I was able to give my wife, Christina, and my stepdaughter, Hannah, this opportunity to tell their story. Christina was a little nervous about being on camera for the first time, and Hannah was too, but being able to share their part of the story firsthand outweighed any hesitation. They could talk about the experience in their own words, and that was very important to them.

The closer we came to our destination, the more nervous the three of us became.

I can honestly say I have never experienced paranormal activity in a vehicle, let alone a moving one. I have seen phenomenal activity from inside a vehicle looking out, but never in it. I have been through a lot and I have witnessed a lot, but a haunted truck was almost laughable.

However, it wasn't the truck that had a mind of its own. It was our devious traveling partner.

Flying down the highway at seventy miles per hour with a tried and proven haunted doll wasn't a good combination to begin with. I should have expected it. We all had a lot on our minds, and every facet of it involved Norman.

An hour out from our destination was enough time for that damned doll to become restless.

We continued on in silence until that silence was abruptly broken. Hannah caused both me and Christina to literally jump and flinch in our seats as she screamed that something had touched her. She swore up and down that it felt like a hand brushing down her arm. I tried to assure her it was probably an insect like a fly or something, but she wasn't convinced.

We were in the middle of that conversation when all of a sudden, the four doors of the truck started locking and unlocking on their own!

Hannah's face turned white, and Christina was scream-ing, "What's going on?"

I looked all around the truck to see what could be caus-ing the locking mechanisms to falter. Christina had the only control to the automatic locks, and I could see her hands were firmly on the steering wheel. I could not immediately see anything else that would cause the door locks to do that, and this went on for a good thirty seconds of confusion. Then, the locking and unlocking just stopped.

The entire truck was quiet, as were we, for moments afterward. None of us said a word to one another. We just stared at the road, all thinking in our own way about what had just transpired. Hannah finally piped up, asking me what the hell just happened.

In my mind, I knew it wasn't just a mechanical mal-function. Deep down, I knew Norman had manipulated the locks. I wasn't going to tell her that for a few reasons.

One, she was already spooked, and two, she was already nervous about the upcoming filming. So I simply told her the cold weather probably caused the locking mechanism to glitch. She seemed content with that idea, so I left well enough alone.

We finally arrived at our hotel without anymore "Nor-manisms." We checked in and settled down for the night before the long day of filming ahead of us the next day. Hannah had her own room, so I'm sure she was happy Nor-man was nowhere near her.

I placed him on the desk provided by the hotel. He wouldn't be bothered for the most part until we headed out to New Dominion Pictures in the morning. We had placed a pillow inside just for the sake of compassion. When I opened the suitcase just to be sure he was still in there, he was already looking right at me.

Norman's suitcase

Peeking out

It was unsettling to see him already peering at me. When we packed to leave for the trip, he was placed on his back in the suitcase. When closed, he was tight against the inner top of the luggage.

I'm not saying he couldn't have shifted and moved during loading and unloading, but it would have taken a great deal of force to do so.

He was now lying completely on his side.

How could he possibly know I would only be peeking in as opposed to opening the suitcase entirely? If he would have remained in the position I left him, he would have been facing up. Weird things to consider. These are things I would have never given a second thought to in the past. But he has accomplished so much over the years, it is hard not to notice every little detail involving him.

I slept well that night. Filming, for me, was always a walk in the park. It never bothered me to actually do it, I just prefer not to. So I slept good. I can't speak for Christina and Hannah, although I can guess their minds raced all that night. We woke up the next morning, got ready, and headed to the filming studio with Norman in tow.

When we arrived, I wasn't really sure of the protocol, so I left Norman in the truck, and we headed straight for the studio's office.

It was simple, we checked in, met the producers, and waited for instructions on filming.

I mentioned to the camera crew that I had brought the real Norman with me. They showed a great deal of excitement and immediately asked me to grab him from the truck. Norman and our story had been quite the talk of the studio since we agreed to go on film about it.

Almost everybody wanted to see the infamous doll that they heard so much about. They wanted to shoot what's referred to as "B-roll" of the doll. For those of you that are unaware of what B-roll is, it's basically extra footage in case you need to fill in a gap during the production.

About the time I was getting ready to run out to the truck, Kelly, our main producer, came back out into the lobby. She asked the camera guys what they were so excited about. They told her. She was not happy. I chuckled when she said, "That 'thing' is not coming in here." So there went that idea, and Norman was brought for absolutely nothing…or so I thought.

We spent the rest of the day filming for the show, and it went really well. We were all very excited to see the finished product, but we had months and months to wait for it to be released. Our episode of *A Haunting*, entitled "Norman the Doll," would air on July 15, 2019, on the Travel Channel.

After finishing for the day, we took Hannah back to the hotel. We then met up with Darren Evans to grab a late dinner at a local restaurant.

As we sat there discussing the filming and the paranormal field in general, we all seemed to go back to one idea. That idea was to film something with Norman that evening. It did not take much convincing.

Christina, Darren, and I decided to conduct an impromptu investigation into Norman back at the hotel. We felt bringing him would have been a waste otherwise, and this would mark the first time he had ever been researched outside of our home.

This was a fantastic idea and crucial to the ongoing research. Would he act the same, worse, or even at all outside of his comfort zone? Did he even have a comfort zone? We were about to find out.

Up until this point, we had never relocated Norman outside of our home to research, and maybe with our guard down a little, Norman would open up more. The three of us finished eating and headed back to the hotel to begin an investigation that would go down in history.

6

Psycho

The level of significance of what happened that night is astonishing and overwhelming. This is when events took a turn for the better (or worse, depending on how you view it). I, for one, haven't decided. But I do know what happened was incredible.

As if the conspiring of Norman prior to this was not enough, there are still things that can amaze this old paranormal researcher. Norman showcased psychic abilities, and I am still pausing in awe at what took place. What occurred that night was something I could have never predicted. In fact, I expected nothing at all in regard to the paranormal.

Instead, what I expected that weekend was an exhausting time of filming and a few beers with an old research colleague. Those things happened, but I also walked away with new knowledge, a newborn excitement, and an invigorating renewal of purpose when it came to furthering my work with Norman. He showed me. He showed us. He demonstrated just how much more to life there was. Norman gave me the book I was waiting to write...again.

From a paranormal researcher's standpoint, he broke the mold and opened the door to a level of understanding I had yet to see from anything supernatural before. This was another example of why I had not just thrown him away when his haunting got out of control. Events like this outweigh the past horrific circumstances.

I am writing this chapter nearly one month after the events that took place. Even so, I am still watching the video, and I am still shaking my head in bewilderment. I am more than pleased not only to have experienced this firsthand, but to know the social media world watched it live from a single, broadcasting cell phone.

I was also filming with a video camera to have a solid copy of the research that was about to take place. Both videos are still readily available to watch on social media. I recommend you check those out to further visualize what actually happened.

Just like Norman Bates, we had our own little psycho in a hotel and, ironically, he, too, was named Norman. So we began setting the stage with multiple cameras running, Norman at the center of attention, electromagnetic detectors, trigger devices, and a live stream for all the world to see. We each had our own methods, so we brought to the table a diverse trio of investigative tactics.

Preparing to investigate

The trigger devices we had in place were lighters and cigarettes. Both of these items give off heat and can burn. We all knew from our own personal experiences and the story of his origin that Norman's very being was rooted in fire.

We figured at this point, knowing the history of Norman and fire, that maybe introducing these objects would amplify his activity. Little did we know at the time just how important they would be.

Everything just seemed to cycle perfectly that evening. It was one of those things that was just meant to be I suppose. We love our work and living the field of paranormal research. It's always smiles and laughter in the beginning. Oh, how quickly those smiles would turn to shocked faces.

I remember saying to my now-wife back in 2008, "Smile! It's four thirty in the morning!" She attended a class I was teaching on paranormal research, and the final exam was an overnight investigation into one of the world's most haunted restaurants.

I always wanted to work with people who had a real passion for the paranormal field. Little did I know then that I would end up marrying Christina. And I certainly didn't know then that we would be raising a haunted doll.

But who were we?

Christina

Christina Lancaster is my communication specialist and empath. Her skills have delivered many very successful investigations, and nobody knew Norman like her and me.

Darren

Darren Evans is one of the best I work with. His knowledge in demonology and deciphering is unmatched in my book. He was the first to ever be brought in on the Norman case outside of Christina and me.

Me

Then there is me, a guy who has lived and breathed the spiritual world since his first experience in 1987. You can say I've been around the block once or twice, and hell, at least I don't look as old as I feel. As always, during the session, this phenomenologist was going to stay behind the camera for the most part.

As we were prepping for the upcoming investigation, we took turns acknowledging the people patiently awaiting the live stream of the work we were about to conduct.

It was approximately eleven thirty in the evening when Darren first launched the live stream on social media. He gave his impressions after physically seeing Norman in the plastic and burnt flesh for the first time. I hit everybody with a brief history on Norman so they could somewhat grasp what we were doing and why. It all officially started with Darren opening the case containing Norman.

Before he even opened the suitcase, Darren insisted on telling us that upon entering the room, he could feel a dark energy coming from the corner. Darren did not know what we had Norman contained in, let alone where he was in the room. So his belief was definitely noted.

Needless to say, upon opening the case, Darren was a little more than taken aback by Norman's presence. He even paused and closed the case just to take a moment to collect himself.

First impressions

I understood where Darren must have been coming from. Norman is a lot to take in. Especially when dealing with him in person.

Darren began laughing hysterically, which I'm assuming was a nervous coping mechanism. But he collected himself well and finally revealed the man of the hour, and the investigation finally began.

Darren added to his initial reaction by stating what he was feeling now was the same as when he first walked in the room. He could sense the energy coming from Norman. He continued by telling us that he was sensing a heat signature coming from the doll, and he couldn't find anything else as the source.

Considering all of Darren's own personal research, he told us that he had never felt anything like this. He even added that he had worked with numerous other allegedly haunted dolls, and none of them compared to Norman.

Investigative work is a lot more than just ghouls and goblins. You have to have a vast knowledge in all things to better conclude on any given case. I pointed out the tear on Norman, the same one I described back in Chapter 2. I wanted to hear Darren's opinion on it, considering the fact that on the side he is one of the best painters I know. Darren examined the doll further and explained for the audience that he had a vast knowledge in glossy paints, satin finishes, and all that painting encompasses. He continued by telling us that the tear on Norman was like nothing he had ever seen before. So he quickly ruled out anything man made. This was the validation I was looking for.

He also noted that the side the tear was on had absolutely no burns of any kind. Darren added once again that this was something he had never seen in a haunted doll before.

The investigation proceeded with Darren making an attempt to communicate with Norman by use of a crystal. Crystals have their own electromagnetism. They can give off vibration frequencies that can affect the paranormal realm in many different ways. The vibrations can control our nervous system and the transmission of information to the brain. This can amplify a person's ability to communicate with a spirit by magnetically placing the human mind and the spiritual realm together. There are plenty of other uses; however, in this case, I have covered what was relevant.

Darren's plan failed or succeeded depending on how far you are willing to go to justify what happened next. As Darren was attempting communication with Norman, without warning, the alarm clock in the room began going off.

Of course, all of our attention was directed toward the sound while Christina was rushing over to investigate the clock. I said aloud, "Please don't tell me that thing isn't plugged in." That would have truly been the icing on the cake. A little shaken, Darren just stared.

Although I was looking in that direction, the camera was not. I turned the camera around just in time to film Christina examining the alarm clock. The clock was plugged in, but there was no tangible reason for the alarm to be sounding off. It was eleven fifty-one in the evening and only twenty-one minutes after we started filming. Our investigation had just begun, and elements in the room were already being affected by Norman.

The time meant nothing to any of us; however, I was thinking that Darren somehow caused a magnetic disturbance between the crystal, Norman, and the alarm clock. It was just too coincidental to consider otherwise. I mean, Christina and I slept in the room the night prior, and the alarm never went off at the time.

Following the alarm clock incident, Darren gave up on the crystal communication and suggested we simply start attempting to get verbal responses from Norman. He kicked off our second attempt to communicate with the doll by asking Norman what he felt inside. Without hesitation, Norman replied, "Afterlife."

All of us were taken aback, amazed and simply dumbfounded by what we had just heard. We were impressed by the fact that the entity was undeniably self aware and knew exactly what plane of existence he was dwelling in.

My research colleague Darren decided to take the investigation up a notch by utilizing one of our designated triggers. Norman had already displayed signs of intelligence, so this was a test to see how far we could take him and what that could achieve. Darren said, "I mean you no harm," as he began flicking his lighter at Norman.

Using a trigger object

Flick after flick after flick as if he was taunting the doll. This prompted Christina to join in. She asked Norman, "Can you blow out the lighter?"

Norman answered.

He said, "No," and I just had to laugh at the look on Darren's face. It was of utter disbelief. He was surprised and impressed all in that single moment.

Darren composed himself once more and said that the flame was triggering more interaction. This was exactly what we had hoped for.

Darren continued firing up the lighter in sequence. One, two, three, four, five more times before Norman responded with, "Your soul."

Darren jumped back in the chair as it scooted on its wheels away from Norman. After reacting unpleasantly, his face looked like he was auditioning for a horror movie. This session was becoming very intense.

Getting responses

Christina pressed on and asked Norman what he thought about me. As if I needed any more reassurance that the little bastard wanted me dead, he replied, "Die."

I sarcastically thanked Christina for asking that question, and despite yet another threat against me, Darren continued on with the lighter experiment. He immediately placed the lighter behind Norman's head and lit it. As soon as he did, Norman exclaimed, "You can't."

Darren instantly pulled his hand away from Norman, expecting something negative to follow that remark. We all sat in pure amazement at the interaction we were witnessing.

Darren spoke up and said, "You guys, this is incredible. The flame is triggering responses."

As Darren put his focus back on the doll, Norman said, "Smile," and he did just that.

Now that the mood was lighter, we decided to flip the script and put Norman back in his suitcase. Darren added to the research by pulling out a crucifix in hopes that this would get a rise out of the main attraction.

Nothing had been planned, as I mentioned, so this caught me by surprise. This was an interesting experiment to see if Norman subscribed to religion or simply used the symbolism as scare tactics.

Using a crucifix as a trigger object

Research is a mixed bag of techniques, personal opinion, and results. Religion is no different. It, too, has its place in this field and can be used either way. It can be used for exactly what it is, or it can be used to rule for or against certain aspects of an investigation. Sometimes religion is used as a defense against the darker spirits while other times it is used to validate the beliefs of an entity. If you learn that a spirit has no preference or loyalty to religion, using it as a defense would be a moot point. On the other hand, if the ghost acknowledges or even fears it, you can use that to your benefit.

Darren placed the cross on top of the suitcase, asking, "What is that?" I was sitting on pins and needles awaiting Norman's response. From inside the case, Norman responded with, "Rage."

"Rage."

Norman's response to the crucifix

All I could hear following that was Christina drawing out, "Oh...My...God."

At this point, that could have meant the thought of religion angered him, or the powers of religion scared him. Either way, the technique was working to further our communication session.

Darren took the cross from atop the suitcase and decided to push the envelope on this tactic and open the case to expose Norman. I've seen some wicked communication sessions, but this one was turning out to be one for the books.

So far, Norman had yet to address the cross other than indicating it enraged him. But that was about to change. A moment after Darren opened the case and brought the crucifix toward him, Norman said, "Hell."

I swear I could write a whole book just about Darren's expressions.

But I digress. Norman had said, "Hell." That was a direct relation to the cross, Christianity, and organized religion. That one word spoke massive volumes. Although it didn't mean Norman feared anything mystical from within religion, it did mean he was educated on the subject. Hell to a cross is like jelly to peanut butter or the devil to Jesus Christ. This meant that Norman was fully aware of what was going on around him. He made sure we knew that fact.

After Darren exclaimed his excitement and awe by saying, "Holy shit," with conviction, we shifted the questioning in an attempt to see what else Norman could recognize. I lit a cigarette and Christina continued to question him. She asked, "Norman, do you smoke?"

Straightaway, he responded with a resounding, "Yes."

Christina took the cigarette from me and placed it on Norman's mouth. After a second or two, the doll reacted and said, "Incredible." We all got a little chuckle out of that one.

"Incredible."

Norman doing standup comedy

Darren just couldn't help himself. He wanted to try more interaction with the flame. It worked before, but I think he wanted to push it to the limit.

Trying the lighter again

It only took one flicker of that flame to get a significant response from the haunted doll. Literally, the second Darren struck the lighter, Norman responded with a reaction none of us saw coming.

Like before, when we brought religion into the research, Norman brought up the Acherontic, the fiercest household name and the most heinous icon ever created. With a flick of that lighter, Norman said, "Devil."

It was hard to determine if he was using those words to scare us or if he was actually saying what he believed. There is a fine line there. I am well educated and versed in many religions, yet I carry myself as agnostic. I know the devil is supposed to be this scary and frightening entity. But to me, he is nothing more than a literary character in the world's most famous book.

Regardless, following that, we decided to turn the lights off. We had yet to really attempt interaction with him in the dark. But before we did, Darren asked Norman if he wanted us to turn the lights out.

The doll had us on pins and needles as we waited for a response. After a few seconds, Norman said, "Light." As you can probably imagine, we turned off the majority of light sources in the room. We were in near pitch black. I personally believed he wanted the light off to create a handicap for us. If we couldn't see, he could take advantage and surprise us much easier.

Darren flicked his lighter and asked the doll when the end of the world was.

"Light."

Norman stating his opinion

Norman randomly said the name "David."

This was completely out of place, we thought. Why would he say a name that had nothing to do with anything relevant to our current situation and the back research? We were in the dark in more ways than one. This was the first time he said something we couldn't somehow relate to him, us, or the case.

We went on with our investigation, and at one thirty-nine in the morning, we all reacted to a sudden knock from inside the room. Of course, we asked each other about it. Nobody had moved, but we all recognized something had shifted in the room.

Now we were documenting physical interaction.

The knock sounded very close to where I was sitting. We were in the dark, so it was nothing more than a personal experience to be logged in the file. There was certainly no way we could validate its authenticity when no one could see anything.

Darren got up from the chair and turned on a single light so we would have a—somewhat dim—view of the entire room. I glanced around my surroundings to see if anything had fallen from a table or desk that could have been the cause of the sounds we heard earlier. Nothing was out of place.

Once the light was turned on, Norman decided to tell us he wasn't resting. He said, "Not resting," and that meant we still had his attention. Darren went back to the chair in front of Norman and sat down. It was time to experiment again. He stuck his hand behind Norman's head and asked him how many fingers he was holding up.

Norman responded with a wise crack. He said, "Ten." We all laughed at the impossible answer. Obviously, Darren doesn't have ten fingers on one hand.

So we took that as Norman cracking a joke or being sarcastic. It was like he was tired of playing these games and answering our questions. But the chances of him stating a number were slim to none. That was still impressive.

Even though I felt Norman was growing tired of the questioning, he still had things in store for us. I continued on and told Norman that he knew who we all were. I told him he knew Christina, he knew me, and he knew Darren.

I was just short of saying all of that when he spouted off the name "Darren." It is both amazing and unsettling to think just how accurate and self-aware the haunted doll was.

If that wasn't enough to let us know he understood, he followed that up with "Parker."

"Parker" is my wife's maiden name. When I first met her in 2008, she was Christina Parker. I guess he addressed me earlier when he said he wanted me to die. That's not a very comfortable feeling.

Norman knows. That's the best way to sum it up.

As we were closing in on wrapping up the investigation, Darren placed Norman back into his suitcase and brought out the lighter once more. Just when we thought it was all over, once again, from inside the case, Norman spoke.

This time he said, "Heat."

The whole night had been a cut above the rest.

However, Norman had one more thing to show us before we called it a night. As everything started to quiet down, our concentration was interrupted by a loud knocking at our door.

All three of us made our way to the door, expecting to see Hannah or somebody who possibly had the wrong room. Everybody knows what somebody knocking on a door sounds like. There is no denying it.

We should have been more ready for what we were about to see, because what we saw was nothing. The extremely long halls made it impossible for someone to have knocked on our door and ran away.

We also noted we had not heard any doors shut following the knocking. Nobody was there.

Norman was showing us the door. In his own way, he was telling us that it was time to cease all investigative work and pack it in for the night.

The investigation took us well beyond midnight as we drew it to a close around four in the morning. Darren still had to do some filming for our *A Haunting* episode in the hours to come, so it was time to call it quits. We ended completely satisfied.

I encourage you all to check out the full video this chapter's screenshots were taken from.[2] Watch the events as they happen and even see a few more occurrences that were not noted here. Just write me on social media, and I will point you in the right direction.

Even so, there was still more to come. Norman did not stop there. He continued on haunting, and it was more than just us. Now he had been touched by Darren and Darren was touched by him. With that came some very disturbing repercussions.

After the fact, we discovered that Darren's dear friend David committed suicide by hanging himself the same night as that investigation. Either the doll predicted David committing suicide, or he was telling us he already had. It was hard to determine with the time of death being so close to our investigation time. It is absolutely crazy to think that Norman could have predicted this or even seen it happening to begin with.

Just how far of a reach did Norman have beyond those who were directly in front of him?

Norman was asked when the end of the world was and around the same time a man was taking his own life. The

2. Stephen Lancaster and Monstervisiontv, "Norman the Haunted Doll AMAZING Investigation 2019," Facebook, Video, February 1, 2019, https://www.facebook.com/monsterVisionTV/videos/60319067012 3645/.

end of the world for Darren's friend was happening, or had happened, and we were clueless.

I cannot say with one hundred percent certainty that Norman had anything to do with that. All I can do is offer you the pieces of the puzzle to form your own image.

We started that investigation all smiles and ended it mourning a tragedy. It was confirmed. Norman was now exhibiting psychic ability. David hanged himself in his own closet. At the time, when Norman said his name, it was a mystery, but not any longer.

We offer much love and respect to David's family.

Darren's dealings with Norman were far from over. Norman was about to show us just how far he was willing to go to show dominance. He was about to show us just how far he *could* go. Darren took a piece of Norman with him, and those pieces created a string of bizarre misfortune.

The next chapter was written by my colleague and research partner Darren Evans.

There is no better person to put into words the series of events that took place after the hotel investigation. Freakish occurrences, and an overload of fear and death, would reign for weeks. The next chapter showcases the evil he experienced following that night.

7

Dead and Grounded

I never did like to fly. There's just something about it that causes my palms to sweat, my blood pressure to elevate, and my heartbeat to quicken. I get a physical reaction just thinking about it. I start thinking about scenarios that perhaps I shouldn't. Like escape routes. I really shouldn't concern myself with them; after all, where are you gonna go once you exit from the airplane?

Am I sitting at the window? Always. Every time I fly, I get the window seat, it's become a given. The Delta flight from Atlanta to Tulsa on January 27 would be no different.

What would be a change of pace, however, would start with the plane catching fire. That was a first. The night before, Stephen and I were engaged in a full-blown investigation of Norman the haunted doll. Nothing was planned, but after unboxing Norman from his vintage suitcase, we all treaded toward macabre events.

Two days following our session with Norman delivered sad news concerning a friend of mine. He had committed suicide. Norman the doll had mentioned his name in the hotel room during our communication session. "Die" was heard coming through a spirit box along with a few other names. A relative contacted me immediately after hearing the news. David had died the same night his name was mentioned by Norman.

I won't go into too much more detail about our session, as I am certain Stephen has already covered it. The investigation ran until nearly four in the morning, and we were able to record some incredible interaction between us and Norman.

We all had to get up early for filming with producers the following morning. Then we had to get back home. So things were a bit hectic when I landed in Atlanta for a two-hour layover.

Those two hours preceded a ten-hour nightmare.

During the layover, my cell phone kept displaying a photo I had taken of Norman. Somehow it had become my android screen saver. At first, I thought it looked kind of cool, but it wasn't something I really wanted to look at getting aboard the Boeing 737 aircraft, which was scheduled to depart at four fifteen in the afternoon for Tulsa.

We crawled onto the tarmac and made a wide turn to position for takeoff. Engines engaged seconds before accelerating. Then without warning, we heard a loud popping sound, and all lights on the plane went out.

Outside the plane behind my seat over the right wing, I saw a plume of smoke. I looked down at my seat to grab my phone for a light, and I once again saw Norman's face on the screen saver.

A wave of fear passed through me instantly.

The lights in the cabin came back on for about ten seconds when another electric popping noise once again was heard. Again, all of the lights went out, and this time no air was circulating in our cabin. The fans had shut down as well.

I was amazed how quickly the air became stuffy and how the temperature rose, making it hard to breathe. Passengers were now speaking out loud, and I wasn't the only one left unnerved.

To my left was an older man who I later found out was a parts engineer for a large corporation who flies twice a week. He commented that he'd never experienced anything like this.

Scenes from the investigation filled my thoughts. Perhaps I shouldn't have held that lighter's flames so close to Norman's already partially melted face. Why did the words "die" and "fear me" repeat so many times during the investigation?

My thoughts were interrupted by a big maintenance vehicle pulling up to the aircraft. He hooked up and began towing the now-lifeless plane back to our gate. The whole process took about an hour.

Power to the cabin was restored after about fifteen minutes, much to our satisfaction, as it really was becoming increasingly difficult to breathe. I kept wondering what would have happened if this electrical failure had occurred in flight? Isn't that what controls the hydraulics that sustain flight?

I began searching internet search engines for aircraft crashes due to electronic failure. That didn't make me feel much better about my situation. I honestly believe that at this point, had I had Norman with me, I would have demanded to be let off the plane. But Norman was with Stephen.

I found myself resetting the screen saver repeatedly to avoid the icy stare from Norman. Yet, each and every time it would return. The captain wired through the intercom that the plane needed repairs and there would be more delays.

People were upset and angry. Everyone was on their phones calling family members. I called my fiancée, Danae, and disclosed the events unfolding. As I was talking to her, I heard her whisper, "Darren, what the fuck," with intensity.

She knew something wasn't right, and after seeing for herself what we accomplished with Norman the night before, she was more than concerned that maybe this was because of him. While all of this was going on, I kept seeing myself using the cigarette lighter to trigger responses from the haunted doll. Every time I did, the doll would utter something like, "no," "die," "fear me," or something else to be viewed in a negative light. I was literally trembling from the whole ordeal.

As a paranormal researcher who has conducted hundreds of Ouija sessions and investigated dozens of haunted locations all over the United States, I had yet to become truly terrified for my life. But now I was, and it was all thanks to that haunted doll. I was becoming sick from anxiety as nausea set in. The next two hours passed by very slowly.

Finally, the captain chimed in that the aircraft had been repaired and cleared for takeoff. That wasn't exactly comforting as we were escorted out to the same runway. I would be lying to you if I said I wasn't praying for safety moments before we were to take off into the dark skies above Atlanta, Georgia.

The prayer was seemingly answered almost immediately. Though not in any way I would have imagined. In an uncanny turn of events, the plane's electrical circuit failed again. This time, no loud popping sound and no ominous grin from Norman peeking through my phone screen.

Just lights out with, once again, no air flow to the cabin.

Passengers had lost patience. I heard an elderly person sobbing. I saw people bowing their heads in quiet prayer. This time it was me exclaiming, "What the fuck?" Fear had turned into anger.

The flight attendants were even showing signs of stress. It was hot and stifling, and I grew very sick of the situation. Within moments, the reserve power kicked in, restoring our lights and temperature control.

I positioned the overhead vent onto my sweaty brow. We were now being told that the plane had been grounded and we would have to board another aircraft with even more delays. I just wanted to go home.

I even said to myself that I couldn't seriously think the doll had anything to do with that incident. Two hours later, we were boarding a different aircraft, and I was once again seated at the window

Every movement, sound, and vibration was quickly analyzed and processed with error expected at every turn in my mind.

Considering what had happened earlier, I was more than paranoid. My brain was on overload, little sleep and maximum weirdness had invaded my world. My fear of flying magnified tenfold.

We crept out onto the runway. As soon as the nose of the aircraft made the final wide turn, we suddenly were thrust back into our seats and into the air in seconds. I honestly expected to crash.

The rest of the flight was fine, other than the recurring haunted thoughts of Norman. Upon arriving in Tulsa, I walked down the aisle to see a red-faced captain standing outside the cockpit. I made it a point to ask him what would have happened if that electrical failure was in mid-flight.

The pilot looked around nervously to see if anyone had heard me. He said it was against policy to speculate. But he did offer to me that in thirty years of military and commercial service, he had never experienced such a loss of power twice in a row like that. The look on his face told me what I needed to know. Strangely, his dark brown eyes reminded me of Norman.

I strolled to the restroom and splashed cold water onto my face. I felt like hell. As I was walking toward baggage pickup, I saw the captain and a flight attendant sitting at a small bar at Tulsa International Airport. I saw three empty shot glasses on their table. I figured the captain was in dire need of a drink. I wanted to join them but my ride was waiting.

But the strangeness with Norman did not stop there. A string of tragic events followed. I woke up the following day to the news that my friend David was discovered dead. I was in shock. He was found dead in his closet. Emergency responders described a horrific scene where he had hanged himself.

A few weeks later, my brother was found nonresponsive and dead at my parents' house.

Within days of my brother's passing, one of my closest friends mysteriously fell from a bridge over Highway 75 in Tulsa. He was pronounced dead on the scene.

It had become beyond weird and head-turning that all of these people just up and died within days of one another. All of these people were tied to me, and I was tied to Norman. I could have never imagined that outcome in a trillion years, but it happened. I became rather lethargic and withdrawn in the days ahead. I had never seen such a series of tragedies unfolding, and I didn't take it well.

A few months passed by, and once again death came knocking. The paranormal world was shocked at the announcement that author Rosemary Ellen Guiley had passed away.

Stephen had shared with Rosemary and me the case file on Norman, and we all communicated back and forth about this crazy doll.

Rosemary was scheduled to assist Stephen and me in the filming of *A Haunting*, but ultimately, she was unable to attend due to illness.

Rosemary was no stranger to haunted dolls and objects, as she documented many cases over the years concerning haunted possessions. Her career spanned five decades, and she held many prestigious honors and active memberships in numerous organizations and specialized fields of paranormal research. As I understand it, her last writings appear in this book.

It's difficult for me to put into words how I feel about all of this. I know Stephen shares with me the sadness of losing a friend, and I know Stephen also salutes Rosemary beside me as we say so long to a paranormal icon. We both agree that whatever Norman touches turns to somberness.

The last time I spoke with Rosemary, she sounded distant and distracted. She told me after thinking about it that she made the decision to step away from the dark side of the paranormal. She had seen all she needed to see with Norman the doll. I told Rosemary in that final conversation that I admired her decision to step away from the darkness. I told her I hope I'm in the position to do the same thing someday.

A fascination with haunted dolls and toys will always be an interest of mine. Perhaps it's the energy we project onto these dolls that determines if they harbor some of the darkness we all have as human beings. I think it's obvious that they are extensions of who we are.

From time immemorial, we have believed that spirits can reside in people, places, and objects. From primitive ghost worship to early voodoo and other extensions that formed the basis for organized religion, spirits are attracted to dolls for the same reason we are.

They can give us comfort and warmth. Dolls bring security to children's insecurities. Or they can inspire fear and terror by attracting energies dark and dangerous.

On one shoulder, there's a voice that says, "No way abhorrent entities can inhabit a doll." The other shoulder whispers, "Oh yes I can, and sometimes I do."

I want to thank phenomenologist Stephen Lancaster for being a great friend and wisely resourceful associate through the years. The Norman case is one for the books, and the material I have seen and witnessed firsthand is not only eye opening but terrific. This is certainly one of the most important paranormal cases currently being researched. It has left an impact on the community and will continue to do so.

8

The Packhouse

What monster lurks inside of Norman? That question remains. It was never a matter of where we would see it again, but more a matter of when. The ionic energy of Hurricane Matthew brought him out once. What could possibly do that again?

The events that took place at the hotel with Norman changed the way I approached paranormal research. I came up with the idea of taking the haunted doll on our investigations from there on out, just to see if that would amplify the alleged activity or open up a new level of communication. I was right on both accounts.

It is well known within the field of paranormal research that spirits utilize man-made energy to affect the atmosphere around you, make sounds, communicate, and even manifest. Up until now, man-made objects have always been the energy source for an entity to feed from. There are cases in which the earth's natural electromagnetism has been the energy source for strange phenomena, but those cases are very rare in the grand scheme of things. Then there are the spirits who have their own energy, and that was what I counted on Norman using.

Now we had a new tool of the trade. That tool was Norman. Now we had a direct line into the spiritual realm. Instead of relying on electronic voice phenomenon or spirit boxes, with the doll, we had our own spirit to do the translating for us. I was hoping spirits in active locations would harness Norman's power and speak through him. What happened at the hotel led me to start using Norman during paranormal field research. The results of those investigations were flat out astonishing. This became the "if you can't beat them, join them" mentality.

Instead of relying solely on electrical items to provide fuel for Norman, why not allow another spirit to do it? After all, that is something we really can't measure currently, so as of right now, the possibilities are endless.

If we were going to try this, the first attempt needed to be at a place we knew had paranormal tendencies. I wanted to waste no time doing it either. I immediately thought of one of our older cases. This case was dubbed "the Packhouse."

The Packhouse

Since 2015, Christina and I have researched the centuries-old, former Haitian slave refuge with incredible results. Located in Warsaw, North Carolina, the old structure was inherited by the McKenzie family and later converted into a secondhand shop to service the needy community.

It is believed the ghost of former Warsaw police chief Michael McKenzie Sr. haunts the historic building. Our research over the years certainly added substance to that belief. During our search there, I personally witnessed a golf club swing from where it was once hanging on a wall.

I also documented a police-issue boot being thrown across the room when I asked the spirit to throw something. More documentation continued over the years to the tune of radios turning off and on, investigators having personal encounters, and even Angela, the wife of Michael McKenzie Jr., being thrown down a flight of steps.

During this time, the McKenzie family were in the middle of renovating the age-old structure. They wanted to turn it into a hangout of sorts for friends and families. They also wanted to make it a base of operations for community benefits.

During the day was fine. I guess it was that old "safety in numbers" thing. Regardless of its purpose, it was never going to be inhabited overnight. The family made that very clear following the attack on Angela. The chief never approved of his son marrying Angela. That quickly became the believed motivation for his attack.

But all of that was neither here nor there for the purpose at hand. The location was packed with spiritually active residual energy, and that was all we needed to know.

I viewed it as lighting a keg of gun powder. It will only explode if gun powder is in it, otherwise the flame is useless. Norman was the light, the Packhouse was the keg, and the ghost of Police Chief McKenzie was the gun powder.

My goal was to fuel Norman with that energy to see if he could intensify his communication and psychic ability so we could learn more about the chief. Essentially, I wanted to see if I could take what he had done at the hotel a step further. I knew there was something dark deep inside of that doll. He chose when and where to come out.

I was growing tired of him having the upper hand. I couldn't even begin to solve the problem without knowing what the problem was. So I had to create more opportunity for him to manifest.

I contacted the McKenzie family about bringing Norman to their location for an experimental investigation. They had followed along with my career. They had also read and seen everything I had to offer with Norman since the beginning.

So it goes without saying the McKenzie family approved.

It had been a little over a month since the hotel incident with Norman. The beginning of March was here, and with that came time to conduct our experiment at the old Packhouse.

Going into it, I wasn't looking for any more validation on the ghost of the chief. I already knew the police chief haunted that location. Focus would be entirely on Norman and seeing if the chief could speak through him.

I guess you could say I needed the rock concert without the band.

This wasn't going to be a "bells and whistles" investigation either. Although we had the majority of our research equipment on hand, the idea was to let Norman run the show, not us.

That night's agenda was simple: meet the McKenzie family at the Packhouse, have dinner, bring Norman, and film the outcome. My plan was to stay behind the camera to make sure everything and anything relevant was properly captured.

We met the McKenzie family at around seven in the evening and began setting up in the bar area of the Packhouse. The renovations that had already taken place provided a long, wooden bar and overhead track lighting.

I placed Norman in the center of the room on the bar. I also set up a stagnant camera to monitor and record the entire session. Joining Christina and me were Michael Jr., Angela, and her brother Chris, who would be appearing in most of the video and images. And of course, Norman was in tow.

For the most part, Michael stood next to me at the side of the bar. Christina was going to handle the majority of the communication session. She was sitting to the right of Chris, just off camera, in front of the bar. Angela stayed firmly behind the bar.

Five people were in that room with one very haunted doll. Chris is a skeptic, but he is also fair and open-minded. He agreed to participate as long as he could be immersed and not just a spectator. I had no issue with his wishes and welcomed the skepticism.

Once everyone and everything was in place, I fired up the camera to begin documenting the first Norman investigation trial. The McKenzie family fired up cigarettes. I figured, Why the hell not? In my studies so far with Norman, fire and smoke seem to be his go-to.

Christina began by introducing everybody to Norman. She followed that up by asking him to let us know if he was in the room. Right on cue, the overhead lights began to flicker. Chris and Angela started staring above them as the ceiling danced like a strobe.

We all glanced around at each other. I could tell the McKenzie family were looking to me for assertion and validation. I gave the nod of acknowledgement to Christina that the communication session had officially begun.

Christina wanted to prove it was Norman that initially made the lights flicker and not some malfunction brought forth by the recent renovations. That was definitely something that needed to be ruled out considering the work that the McKenzies were doing inside. She continued and asked Norman to make the lights flicker again.

Norman makes the lights flicker

Immediately, the lights above us began pulsating in and out. Every one of us focused on the ceiling. The room looked like a rave was taking place with how abundant the lights bouncing off and on were. As the lights in the room continued to flash, Christina asked Norman what he thought of Chris.

In an instant, Norman responded by calling him an "idiot." We couldn't keep from laughing because it caught us all off guard and was a spot-on description. Chris is the self-appointed clown when he wants to be. He is known for his silly antics and being the life of the party. So it came as no surprise that Norman referred to him as such. It was incredible to witness such a personal and intelligent response from the doll.

The tone of the room was serious up until that point, but none of us could contain the continued laughter. Even Norman recognized that fact.

He said, "You laugh," as if to let us know he was aware of what was going on in the room.

While we were still laughing, Angela decided to see if placing a crucifix in Norman's lap would have any effect on his responses or activeness.

The ambience in the room reverted back to its original, serious tone after Norman responded to her actions. Norman exclaimed he was afraid upon Angela placing that cross on his lap.

I immediately started thinking back to the hotel investigation with Christina and Darren. Any time we would introduce something that was rooted in religion, Norman would respond appropriately. The session at the Packhouse was proving to be no different. Norman once again was exhibiting disdain toward the crucifix. This might lead one to believe that Norman was in fact a demon, and that is a strong possibility. But at the same time, even the nicest, most innocent, and loving religious person fears God's wrath.

We continued to watch and listen for the next little outburst from the haunted doll. Just when the room was starting to become uncomfortably quiet, Norman spoke again. This time he was making it clear that the cross was unwelcome, and he knew exactly who to blame for it.

"Angela."

Norman's response to the crucifix on his lap

Angela gasped and stepped back from the bar when she heard Norman say her name. She stared at me through the camera in befuddlement while removing the cross from Norman's lap. I think she was seeking out some sort of comfort from me with that look of fear on her face. But there wasn't anything I could provide her. I was just as stunned. Christina and I were witnessing and learning about this situation right along with her.

There was no question about it at this point. Norman knew what was going on. His clever and relevant responses clearly removed any doubt about that. So far, everything that I documented echoed the activity at the hotel. Norman once again proved to be self-aware. He described Chris. He called us out for laughing. He even addressed Mrs. McKenzie by her first name.

However, I wanted more than that. I needed something to happen that would help solidify the notion that he also had psychic abilities. All of his communication revolved around us. Not one time did he mention or even allude to the supernatural forces that already existed in the building. Certainly that was interesting to note, but again that's not why we were there. I was hoping for a glimpse into the police chief's haunting to prove the doll's ability. Instead, something just as credible occurred.

Chris shocked us with what happened next. He can be a hard case sometimes. Chris is very skeptical when it comes to reported paranormal phenomena. I believe he did what he did hoping the test would fail just so he could say, "I told you so."

Instead, what happened caused a very vocal person to become nearly speechless. I have to admit that I had never seen anything quite like it. Norman would prove the impossible possible.

The room was quiet again, and this was when Chris decided to take the lead in a very creative way. He grabbed his cell phone and chose a picture that only he and Norman could see.

Chris asked Norman, "Who is that? Who is that in the picture?"

Time just seemed to slow down altogether during this part in our communication session.

I was patiently and eagerly anticipating what Norman would say or do to the questions Chris proposed. I think we all were. Silence engulfed the room as I sat on the edge of my seat behind the camera.

Angela stared toward Norman and Chris. Christina remained still in her seat behind Chris. Michael and I stared intently into the camera monitor. Chris asked the question again as he held the photo right up to Norman. I could tell he was getting a little frustrated. Norman had been unresponsive since he called out Angela.

Chris continued to hold his cell phone where Norman could see it. The doll just stared and stared. Finally, right when I was about to change the direction of the session, Norman spoke up. He said only one word. He said, "Jacob."

That name meant nothing to me and Christina. But the reaction from Chris said everything. Immediately following Norman's response, Chris nervously and enthusiastically said, "Wow."

This part of the investigation went down so fast and all at once. I was wondering what the hell blew his mind like that. Chris spoke up and said that he showed Norman a picture of his son Jacob. Christina and I never even knew Chris had a son, let alone one living all the way up in Virginia. This further added to Norman's credibility after tapping into a child over a state away.

I blurted out, "Are you serious?"

I don't know what satisfied me more. The fact that Norman legitimately answered the question correctly or the baffled and impressed look on the face of a now-convinced skeptic. It was safe to say that Chris walked away a believer that night.

I walked away with yet another fragment of Norman's universe. Once again, the doll showed us a level beyond basic communication and understanding. Once again, he demonstrated a psychic power.

I can't say for sure whether or not the residing spiritual energy played a role, but I can say the doll delivered beyond expectations. From the hotel to the Packhouse, Norman demonstrated he could use the energy of whoever is around him as a network into all relative elements.

What are the chances of a doll being haunted? What are the chances of a haunted doll being able to look at a picture and tell you what it is? I would say, very slim to both questions. Everything I was looking at so far with Norman broke all of the rules.

That's the beauty of this field. It is never ending and forever evolving. There is always something new to observe and learn from. I thought the experiment at the Packhouse would have been enough to satisfy my curiosity. But hell, how could I possibly stop there?

I had been given that once-in-a-lifetime shot when Norman came into our lives. Why quit now? I had stumbled upon a unique entity with uncharted attributes.

I admit looking back that I became very obsessed with that doll. However, I still had yet to bring out of Norman what I wanted to see. I wanted to see that dark entity from 2016 again or the creepy, old passerby in our house from last Christmas.

I was still looking for a source. I was still trying to prove that Norman feeds off of the spiritual realm. I needed to see the big, bad wolf inside of Norman. There needed to be a level of certainty added to the equation. My theory was to place him in spiritually active locations to ignite the monster within.

The Packhouse succeeded on many levels but failed to produce anything beyond the smiling plastic of the doll. Little did I know, the answer would be right next door.

9

Won't You Be My Neighbor?

Not everybody can say they've had real estate agents ask them to stay in their house when showing the property next door.

For years, the house right next door to us remained empty. It had long since degraded with the grass all grown up. Weeds and vines strangled the abandoned house, and not a peep from that location had been heard in years.

The bank struggled and struggled to sell the tainted property.

Finally, after a year of being on the market, they started bringing in landscaping crews to at least make the outside look presentable. They even asked me to keep out of sight when they showed the house. The real estate agents were aware of Norman, the first book, and the television appearances I made over the years.

The people of my town knew me well. A couple times a year, I would appear in the local newspaper for something or other involving the supernatural. In retrospect, I understand their manner of concern. I guess they didn't want perspective buyers freaked out by the possibility of a guy involved so heavily in the paranormal becoming their next-door neighbor.

Plus, I have the tendency to go outside naked.

Big Steve came along in October of 2018 and bought the place. He and his wife had been living out of a camper at that point. He didn't really know what he was getting into by moving next door to us. Frankly, *we* didn't know what *he* was getting into until he moved next door to us.

I highly doubt he thought he would be controlling a burning barn in our backyard or talking to a haunted doll months from then.

But he did.

Big Steve acquired the property dirt cheap. A man had died in it back in 2016, and with the full disclosure law, that wasn't something real estate agencies could keep secret. It was a hard sell, especially considering how rundown the property had become in the past two years.

But Steve bought it regardless, with full intentions of fixing it up. He had dreams of grandeur until he realized it was haunted. His wife started hearing and seeing things that spooked her to the point of never going back in the house.

Big Steve and I quickly became good friends and neighbors to one another. Over the months, he had heard plenty of stories from me concerning the paranormal. I knew something wasn't sitting right though. I never saw them in the house all that much. They were always outside or in their camper.

After nearly six months of living out of their camper in the front yard, Steve confided in me about the strange occurrences in their house. He said the activity began shortly after they started ripping up old carpet and redoing one of the bathrooms. Big Steve added that his wife had odd and overwhelming feelings come over her in the house. During renovations, she even claimed to have seen a small board fly across one of the rooms.

In April of 2019, he asked me and Christina to have a look inside the empty home to see if we could determine what was causing the haunting or rule it out altogether. He wanted an answer one way or another. My gears started turning, and I once again saw an opportunity to use Norman.

Unlike the Packhouse, I had no clue what waited inside. For all I knew, there could have been nothing at all and the whole thing was all in their minds. But Big Steve's wife refused to move into the home until something was done. She was terrified.

I wish I could say we helped in the matter, but I think we actually made things much worse.

Well, Norman made things much worse. Christina and I knew that Norman was most likely the cause of the activity at our neighbors' house. If it wasn't him, maybe Norman would lead us to whatever it was.

Years ago, when other people lived next door, we never heard a peep about a haunting. Of course, somebody did die in there. But considering what we knew about Norman, it was easy to assume he was the culprit. So we felt a little obligated to check out our neighbors' house.

We decided to take an evening to explore Big Steve's house and case. For us, it was a luxury having a new case right next door. We could research it pretty much anytime we wanted to.

That evening, Christina and I gathered up all of our research gear, and alongside Norman, met Big Steve on his porch. His wife remained outside in their camper during the entire investigation. She wanted no part of it.

The main door to the house was an offbeat color of red. In many ways, that was menacing looking to begin with. A guy dies in the house. The front door is red. New tenants discover it's haunted. Norman lives next door. I couldn't complain. All the components of interest were there. I just figured it was the minds of two individuals that were just trying to get accustomed to their new home, and the creaks and cracks were playing tricks on them.

Once we were able to get inside and set up, the house began to speak. We were standing in the kitchen, where we set up our base of operations, when I heard something from across the house move.

It was evident to me that the sound came from the far back room. Initially, I thought maybe a rat was the culprit. Whatever it was definitely sounded like something heavy moving across the floor. I wasn't getting too excited just yet.

Norman was set up for the time being in the kitchen with ionic testers surrounding him.

Ionic testers light up when electromagnetic fields or ionic energy is nearby. This could mean a spirit is in the room if no mechanical device is the reason for activating them.

Human beings give off their own ionic energy. Every living thing does. So as long as we aren't close to them, any light documented could be significant.

Once we were ready to begin, Christina once again led a communication session. She began by asking Norman what the sound was I heard in the other room just moments prior. Norman answered, "Your hell."

I would be lying if I said that little bit of foreshadowing wasn't intimidating. I could hear Big Steve behind me exhale a barely audible, "Wow," as he tried to catch his breath.

Wow was just the common word used around Norman. I think Steve might have been slightly regretting moving forward with this investigation.

There was barely any breathing room in between Christina's question and Norman's answer. There was hardly an inkling of space in between Norman's answer and the loud crash that came from the back room again, startling us all. Norman knew whatever was in the house was in that back room. So right from the start, Norman was bringing out that house's baddy. With all of our focus toward the back room, Norman decided to get our attention again.

He said, "Talk to me." He knew our attention was elsewhere as we discussed the ongoing loud noises from across the house. Sometimes they sounded like something scuffing across the floor, while other times they sounded metallic.

We continued by getting Norman to participate with us even further. Christina asked him if he wanted to go into what we were calling the "dark" room. This was the area all of the unexplained sounds were coming from.

The doll firmly said, "Now."

"Now."

Norman wants to go to the "dark" room

My theory was starting to become more than just a theory. It was becoming a reality. Norman was recognizing the fact that something else was in that house other than the four of us. There were many questions racing through my mind. Was Norman going to use that spiritual energy, and was this investigation going to finally reveal something we had never seen before?

The three of us and Norman relocated to the doorway of the dark room. We placed the doll at the edge of the entrance. The next series of events happened so fast, we were all extremely disoriented.

It would take reviewing my camera to fully comprehend and take in exactly what had transpired. Filming commenced, and so did the phantom sounds. This time it sounded like a hammer on metal. I jumped and looked at everybody. I was asking, "Did you not hear that?" with intense excitement over and over.

Norman watching the investigation heat up

Within that darkness, something evil was lurking and waiting for just the right moment to catch us off guard. I am not sure if Norman knew that, was that, or delivered that. Before the excitement could calm down, more loud and bizarre sounds came from within that room.

Norman spoke up and said, "Burns."

Burns was not a comforting word coming from him. I couldn't help myself. That crazy, inquisitive side just came bursting out of me.

In a brief moment, I lost myself, and I told Norman to show us where the man was.

Our situation was escalating and becoming more and more intense. I, of course, was referring to the ghost of the house or the entity inside of him. At the time, I would have been happy with either one. Norman instantly replied with a snarky remark. "Why should I?"

I'm not sure whether he said that to be sarcastic or he said that to prove he could. Either way, what occurred scared the living shit out of every single one of us. A split second before anything happened there was one last, immense, booming sound before an exceedingly accelerated and off-the-wall looking anomaly shot out of the dark room behind Norman and directly at us. It only lasted for a split second, and whatever it was did not make impact with any of us, but it happened so shockingly fast that I stumbled to the ground. Big Steve and Christina were forced backwards.

The speed of the anomaly exceeded the frame rate of the camera I was using. I was only able to capture and document a few frames of it. I saw the same exact thing with my own two eyes.

The elongated shape could have been attributed to its incredible speed. Maybe it wasn't long at all. It just appeared so due to moving so fast. It looked similar to light trails or something you see in an overexposed photograph of automobiles traveling at night.

Only this thing did not look like a light source at all. This thing had its own unique texture and hue. It had a lifeless, grimy, desert sand type surface. It is just a blur on the camera, but there is enough to show you that something was there. Something had flown out of that room and toward us. It unfortunately happened so fast that all we had for documentation purposes was a brief and blurry image.

Of course, between the speed of the anomalous movement and me falling backward with the camera, a clear shot just wasn't happening. But there was no denying that something had come out of that room and did so at great speed.

That was enough for Big Steve to call it quits.

We all had seen something come barreling out of that room. We just didn't know what that something was. We all knew that, due to its size, it wasn't anything like an insect flying by. I mean, this thing was a good four feet long. But

Big Steve did not want to look into it any further. What we witnessed rattled him. He said he had seen enough, so Christina and I took our cue to call it quits on the investigation. We weren't really sure what to tell Big Steve. So we left well enough alone.

We all saw that anomaly fly out from behind Norman. But was it what was haunting his home, or was it completely related to Norman the doll? It was hard to say. But Big Steve had never seen anything like that before in the house up until that night.

I added the image to the Norman file as an unexplained anomaly. Still to this day, Big Steve and his wife have not moved into that house.

The next three months were silent as far as Norman was concerned. He sat content in his glass coffin in our bedroom. Our house could not have been any more normal at that point. I was beginning to think that maybe taking him out on investigations with us doubled as some sort of peace offering. Yet what we saw at Big Steve's house told a different tale.

I never did like the calm before the storm. I always found it to be more frightening with all of the wonder and anticipation of what is hiding behind the blanket of somberness. The next big occurrence that was about to take place would shock not only me but my entire family and dear, close friends.

A few sentences on social media about suicide rocked my entire network online and off and changed my life forever. I was about to become a pawn in another one of Norman's demented games, and this time, he won.

10

A Suicide Solution

July 7 of 2019 will go down in history as yet another close call with death at the hands of the paranormal. When the doctors can't explain it, you have no choice but to think beyond modern medicine and science.

Norman was determined to get me out of the picture one way or another. Between the death threats and near misses, I thought I had seen it all. He tried to kill me in 2016. He tried to burn us all alive in 2018. He made countless verbal threats over the years with multiple attempts to force me to leave.

Norman had succeeded where he had failed so many times over the years. I just don't know how else to explain it. I had no part in it. It all just happened and so fast. It was just as much of a shock to me as it was to everybody else. The doll got rid of me.

When I woke up that morning, I did not expect to end up sleeping somewhere else. Nor did I expect to see an outpouring of monsters that I've researched over the years.

I arose early that day like I did any other. I woke up around four thirty, took all of our dogs outside, then slowly started my day. That Sunday morning, Christina and Hannah left for the beach. It was about seven in the morning when they headed out for their hour-long drive to a day in the sun.

I, on the other hand, opted to stay home. I am not much of a beach guy. I decided I was going to take the day and work on the backlog of cases that had been stacking up since the whole Norman debacle.

I was still juggling my normal paranormal case load on top of the home field research with our haunted doll. Norman would remain in his case sitting on top of my desk as I worked.

Most of that early morning is as clear as day to me as I recall it. While thirty minutes of it has been lost to the abyss of time. The last thing I remember doing that morning was opening up one of my case file drawers to pull out a folder on an old hotel I had investigated. The next thing I remember was my neighbor Big Steve screaming in my face. If you are confused, just know, so was I. I still am.

Big Steve had found me asleep on my bed after he rushed into the house. But why he rushed into my house was the big question. During the thirty minutes in which I had blacked out, a message on my behalf had been spread across all of social media.

Now this was no ordinary message. This was a suicide note. Apparently, I had, without knowing, typed a short suicide note on my social media profile. At least that is what everybody thought. The note was posted online at just before ten in the morning.

"It wasn't murder. I killed myself. I wanted to do it in the cornfield but instead I am in bed with my dogs. I wish I could have kissed you one more time Christina. I love you all."[3]

My family and friends were all in a panic to get to me. Upon seeing the message, my wife and stepdaughter immediately left the beach to come home to me. My wife knew something wasn't right, and this was completely out of character for me.

Christina had called Big Steve from the beach. She asked him to go check on me after she saw the message pop up online.

Big Steve was also concerned because, apparently, he had received an email from me requesting a gun near the same time as my social media post. I had done none of this, but somehow it had all been done.

When Big Steve woke me up, I was beyond startled, surprised, and dumbfounded. I had no clue as to what was

3. The note has since been removed and is no longer publicly available.

happening other than what was happening right in front of me. Steve was yelling, "Are you okay? Are you okay?" very frantically.

I assured him I was, and he said that everybody was really worried about me. I asked him why, and he told me what had happened within the past thirty minutes. I couldn't believe what I was hearing.

This is something that, in any state of mind, I would never do. It just isn't me. It isn't in my character nor my personality. I don't believe in suicide. I had never been suicidal before in my life, let alone acted on it.

I tried to convince my neighbor that everything was alright and that this was just one big misunderstanding. He wasn't buying it, nor was he going to take the chance. But something else wasn't right.

I felt extremely dizzy and lightheaded. I could feel my heart pounding through my head. It was like a tribal drum machine marching to a requiem. An overwhelming sickness came over me. It was reminiscent of a few years ago when I was taken down by what could only be described as a heart attack. That, too, was at the hands of Norman. Something wasn't right with my health.

Big Steve called Christina to assure her he found me alive. He found me spirited but not well. I was spirited alright. Christina arrived at the house, but not before calling an ambulance.

Before Steve dragged me out of the house, I glanced up at Norman in his case. I knew he was the immoral engineer behind all of this. With my eyesight the way it was at that time, I had to have seen a hundred of him. It was like I was looking through the eyes of a fly.

I threw my arm over Big Steve's shoulder, and he walked me out of the house to where Christina was waiting with the truck. I couldn't walk so he was dragging my feet. The pain was severe, and the whole world was spinning through my eyes.

Big Steve helped me climb into the truck. Christina was not going to wait for the ambulance to arrive. She was going to arrive at the ambulance. We flew down the highway toward the hospital, which was thirty minutes away.

I was coming in and out of consciousness the entire drive. I felt like I was out of my body looking back at myself. It was the most surreal, unnatural feeling.

Christina called the police, and they caught up to escort us to the coming ambulance. About fifteen minutes later, Christina met the ambulance at a local business in town. None of this I remember. I was educated on everything that happened after the fact.

I was transferred from the truck into the ambulance, and the paramedics took me the rest of the way to the hospital. My vital signs were off the charts. My blood pressure was logged at 280 over 138. This had death written all over it. I was beyond stroke level and very close to taking my last breath on this earth.

At the hospital, I regained consciousness as they ran intravenous fluids and drew blood for immediate lab work. With my wife being a former nurse, I have learned a lot over the years when it comes to the medical field. What was happening wasn't good by any definition.

They were prepping me for a stroke.

Up until this point, I had never been a candidate for such a thing. I had always been of the utmost good health. In recent years, that utmost health had a few hiccups in its record thanks to the paranormal field.

The medical staff were doing everything in their power to level me out and prevent me from dying. They were also taking the necessary precautions and conducting the necessary tests for an attempted suicide. The staff were misled. Misled like everybody else by something I never even attempted to do.

I stared off in a daze as nurse after nurse poked and prodded. It was all like an extremely bad and realistic nightmare. Everything happening around me appeared to be in slow motion.

All of the murmuring voices from the staff and family and friends made them seem like they were coming from miles away. That whole day is one big blur. Between the foggy bright white lights, the lab coats, the needles, and confused state, I felt like I had been beamed aboard an extraterrestrial mother ship for some sort of species testing.

Imagine your eyes constantly blurred. Those of you who wear glasses, I am sure can relate. Imagine your eyes full of water constantly. Not physically but visually. Imagine all of this going on around you, and you can't make any clear sense of any of it. Everything is indistinct.

It was a nightmare I could not wake up from.

With every passing nurse, I desperately attempted to convince them that this was a big mistake and I was not suicidal. None of them would listen.

It seemed at the sight of that social media post and the email to my neighbor concerning a gun, all points of authority just shut down to my pleading. They had regulations to adhere to and laws to follow. A written suicide threat was grounds for being committed until doctors could clear you. They must feel you are not only in a frame of mind to be safe alone but also safe to others.

I couldn't believe what I was hearing as the nurses and doctor spoke. It was like I wasn't even there. I didn't exist as a person. Instead, I was only a procedure and an act of protocol. The very person they thought they were going to help was the very person they refused to listen to.

I became angry and lashed out at the nurses for ignoring my testimony. They just didn't want to hear it. They refused to. I repeatedly told them I did not want to kill myself. I gave every reason in the book not to. I told them

I was a successful writer, had a wonderful family and lots in store for the future. I told them my life was perfect.

It didn't matter. All of that fell on deaf ears. I lost all human rights the moment that social media post was made. Once they researched me and my career, things went even further in the wrong direction. As accepting as our society has become with paranormal entertainment and research, their judging was a step backward in time. I felt like I had become a victim of a modern-day witch hunt. By their logic, every one of you reading this belonged there with me. Any interest in the paranormal was a red flag for them. That kind of talk was crazy.

They sedated me as they struggled to get control of my blood pressure. My anger was not helping in that department. They were going to commit me for the suicide threat in addition to monitoring my uncontrollable blood pressure. They made attempt after attempt to level my blood pressure out, yet nothing was working.

My drug screening had returned, and I was clear. I knew I would be, but they didn't. They could not blame drug use for my believed behavior, which confused them further. They committed me. I was put on lockdown and isolated from society.

That evening they relocated me to a room at the top of the hospital. A nurse was to be stationed at my door every hour of every day. My vitals were to be monitored every hour of every day.

I had become a prisoner on the brink of dying. I had never felt so helpless in my life. All I could think about was Christina back home, and that doll just sitting there scheming further. He had won for now.

Sunday, July 7, would be the last time I would see the sun and feel its warmth until being released over a week later. I was isolated in a very small room that had only a mattress and a toilet in it, but not before being stripped naked and forced to wear paper-like clothing.

Mental illness is a serious condition. There are people out there who truly need help, and there I was involuntarily monopolizing a spot that could have gone to a person needing it. And the place definitely wasn't for me. That certainly doesn't mean it isn't the appropriate place for healthcare, but I think I was suffering from a bit of claustrophobia.

The one and only window was barred. There were no paintings, television, or electronics of any kind. It was a dingy white prison cell that screamed "institutional." I was on the same floor with violent convicts, people with severe mental disorders, and desperate, drug-addicted individuals. It was the scariest, most desolate place I had ever seen or been. I lived in fear the entire time.

You could walk in there with nothing wrong with you and walk out a very changed and disturbed person. The place actually caused post-traumatic stress disorder as they stuck my arm with needle after needle, administering medication in an attempt to convince me that the problem *was* me. The scariest part was knowing I didn't really need to be there, and having no control of the situation perpetuated that fear. This was a point I brought up every day upon seeing the doctor.

I repeatedly told him that I was fine and this was a case of mistaken belief. I told him the only thing depressing, scary, and traumatic was that very place. I was an unwilling lab rat. I was being treated for something I did not have, and with that came horrific repercussions. I embarked further down the rabbit hole and met all of my demons at once.

11

The Doll Made Me Do It

What was I going to do? Causing a scene and screaming that a haunted doll had been attempting to kill me certainly would not have been the wisest thing to do considering the circumstances. That bastard knew it.

I was already getting stares for believing in the paranormal. There was an irony to that. It aggravated me to no end when I would later have discussions with nurses about their paranormal experiences. Yet I seemed judged for believing it.

Considering the nature of this chapter, it is well beyond crazy to think a possessed toy caused all of this. I have no other choice but to believe so. I did not attempt suicide. I did not threaten to. It all had been done in my name without my knowledge.

What happened next was all a direct result of the medication they were giving me. I refuse to believe otherwise because let's face it, any other reason beyond science in this case is just too unbelievable. But it happened.

I think I was seeing what I had seen so much over the past two decades. It was almost like every paranormal case I had ever worked came spiraling down into that room and was very much alive. I know it to be true because I interacted with the nurses that night, and they confirmed it all the next day. I do have to say I could see a lot of question and hesitation in their eyes. Part of me believed they were starting to see I didn't have anything wrong with me.

They knew who I was and what I did. They had seen the *A Haunting* episode while I was on lockdown. One nurse in particular even said she saw me in the local paper that day. I had no idea I was even going to be in the local paper. It was an article on Norman the doll and the show I had just appeared on.

Part of me believed the staff actually considered this whole situation, from the suicide post on social media to me visually reliving paranormal memories, to be something paranormal. Part of me believed they were just humoring me.

My blood pressure resolved itself about three days into my stay. The doctor could not explain such a quick and drastic change in it. I could. But it wasn't something I was going to tell them.

I have always been a subscriber to "spiritual magnetism." It's a theory I came up with nearly a decade ago. I believe that when a person is exposed to spiritual energy for long periods of time, they become spiritually magnetized. This state can lead one to be more in tune with the spiritual realm and it more in tune with you.

It's like when you vigorously rub a paper clip across a magnet and it becomes temporarily magnetized. For a short time, it can pick up other paper clips. But eventually it loses its magnetism.

If you take a person like me who is constantly exposed to spiritual energy, it is easy to believe just how spiritually magnetized I could become. This is my job. This is what I do for a living.

With that being said, I believe that Norman did something to me that Sunday morning to cause my body to go into overload. Maybe if I stayed at home, I would have died; because after a few days of being away, my body leveled out.

To be honest, I believe that his spiritual grip on me dissipated because I was gone. Maybe he knew that it would and that's why he went out of his way to set me up for getting committed.

The blood pressure situation was one problem out of the way. The only one left was being locked up for something that simply wasn't true. But I had to prove that. In order to prove that, I had to play by their rules and pretty much just manipulate them with their own game.

But that wasn't going to be easy when they were medicating me to the point I was losing touch with reality. That is definitely the downside to being medicated for something you don't need. It is like when Ritalin is prescribed to someone with attention deficit hyperactivity disorder (ADHD). They calm down. That's the drug's purpose. But when you prescribe it to somebody who doesn't actually need it, they become hyperactive.

The doctor had put me on antipsychotics. The only problem was, I did not need them.

On Wednesday night of that week, I took a trip into the darkest paranormal realm: the one located inside my head. It was all so vivid. I will never forget it.

Nine in the evening was medication time, and lights-out was at nine thirty that night. I crawled on top of my mattress and just stared at the ceiling. Shortly after, I could notice the sounds of the ward registering differently. I was starting to slip into a hallucinogenic coma. It was a coma, yet I was very much awake.

The experience started off subtle. At first, I found myself watching my hands as electricity bounced back and forth between them. At the time, I thought this, and the events to come after, were really happening.

Then I started to notice the entire room become engulfed in electrical, blue pulsating webs. They looked like electrified spiderwebs. At that moment, I saw something moving from behind the toilet. For the first time in my life, I was actually petrified at the sight of something paranormal.

It was a young, short-haired white boy in an all-black suit emerging from behind the toilet. He was possibly six years old. Even though he was not intimidating, I was frozen in fear. I was paralyzed from the drugs I had just taken.

Nothing is scarier than seeing something like that and being unable to move or react or scream out for help. He just stood there looking at me, slightly swaying back and forth.

I recognized him from a dark case I took over fifteen years ago involving a little boy who had drowned. It was him. He had been chased to a pond in the middle of a field by an unseen force. That force kept him paddling for his life in the middle of the pond. Eventually, his body gave out and he drowned.

Before I could really grasp what was going on around me, the blanket of electrical webs paved the way for a young white girl in a dirty gray nightgown standing near my feet at the bottom of the mattress. Her long black hair swayed in time with the little boy's motion. She appeared to be about ten years old.

Like the boy, I recognized her from an old case. She was Emily. She was the little girl who was raped and murdered by her father during World War II. Her wooden box, with her little dress and a few select toys, is still in my house to this day.

My focus shifted to the right toward the barred window. Outside of it stood a young black woman. She was desperately trying to communicate with me. I could hear no words. All I could see was her mouth moving up and down as she tried to talk.

She was killed in a bus accident years ago just outside of an elementary school that I investigated numerous times.

I continued lying there. The room started to close in on me. Outside, it began to snow. It began to snow in July. I leaped from the mattress, picked it up, and threw it across the room in an attempt to break the haunting cycle of my past.

A nurse came running in, screaming at me. She kept screaming for me to calm down. I ran out and down the hall with an orderly chasing me. I kept yelling out to the other nurses that I had to get out of there. I was screaming about everything I had just seen.

These are the things I can remember. What I couldn't remember was told to me after the fact by the head nurse the following day.

Apparently, I had attempted to escape through the nurse's station. I had ripped my bedsheet to shreds and attempted to make a phone call to my wife with an imaginary cell phone. I had even claimed to have met with deceased family members during that episode.

Was any of it true? The hallucinations and the stories they represented were certainly true. I guess those drugs brought out the ghosts living within my psyche.

The next morning, the nurses on staff that previous night reported to the doctor what had transpired. I was instantly taken off of the anti-psychotics. I had suffered from adverse effects according to the doctor. I thought I would be in the clear at that point and get released. Unfortunately, they were still going to continue monitoring my blood pressure, and their eyes were still focused on that suicide letter.

After five more days of playing patient, the doctor gave the order. Finally, after eight total days, I was able to convince the doctor I was not suicidal. I played by their rules, said everything I knew they wanted to hear, and just manipulated the game. That came easy. I just told the truth.

The truth, that is, minus the whole crazed haunted doll part. I put my ego aside, allowed the anger to calm down, and just went through the motions so they would see their mistake.

It was pretty much like you see in the movies: strict, close quarters and a lot of uncertainty due to some of the more violent patients. Like I said, it was the scariest place I had ever been. I feared for my life in there. I can only imagine what happens over a longer period of time in a place like that. Just in the small amount of time I was in there, multiple fights broke out, blood was splattered across the hall, a man committed suicide in a place that's supposed to be impossible to do so, and another man somehow managed to catch his mattress on fire.

But thankfully, after a week and a day, I returned home. I was discharged with no further instructions. The doctors could not diagnose me because there wasn't anything to diagnose. They did, however, prescribe me blood pressure medicine and recommended I follow up with a doctor about that.

As far as the suicide, they chalked that up to misinterpretation on behalf of my neighbor.

By law, they had to keep me for as long as they did. Suicide threats are not to be taken lightly, and when one was blasted over social media for all the world to see? Well, that draws attention. At the time, I figured I would manipulate them at their own game so I could be released. Since then, I have recovered from that experience and my views have changed. I no longer hold a grudge against the hospital or its staff. They simply did what they had to do.

This, by far, was the hardest chapter for me to write. It isn't easy letting the world know about something such as this. Especially concerning a subject matter so sensitive. I assure you that I am fine. Everything has been fine with me and the family ever since (aside from Norman). It is almost like it never happened at all.

I lay in bed at night and cringe at the thought of being locked in that place again. It was horrible. It was prison. I could not stand having no control over anything. I was so concerned for my family. If something were to have happened, there would have been nothing I could have done about it. But I was home. I was free. I was back to doing what I always did.

It didn't come easy facing Norman after all of that. But I had to. However, I debated within myself as to whether or not to include this chapter. It may be a little presumptuous to say, but there will be a handful of people who read this and claim it is all bullshit from a crazy paranormal guy who got locked up in a psych ward. Others will read it and possibly understand because they, too, have been there.

You probably don't realize how many people I spoke to and how many crazy stories I heard while I was in the hospital. The funny thing is, considering my line of work, I hear stories like that all of the time, sometimes much worse. None of those people are sleeping in a psych ward.

If you don't live the field, you cannot possibly begin to understand it. But I seek the truth. Always have, always will. Ultimately, I decided for this chapter's inclusion because I would have been cheating you otherwise. It's part of Norman's story.

Three days after being discharged from the hospital, my good friend and research colleague Rosemary Ellen Guiley passed away suddenly at the age of sixty-nine. Another person in my life related to Norman now gone. My happiness about being home quickly turned to sorrow upon hearing the news.

I went into the hospital thinking about Norman, and I came out of it thinking the same. It was time to attempt another communication session with the doll. And Norman? He was about to shine again.

12

I'm Still Here

It had been quite some time since I had attempted a communication session within our home. For a while, all of the activity was sparked by Norman without any prompting from us. So, for the sake of documentation, I decided to take yet another opportunity to reach out to the malevolent spirit.

I wanted to let Norman know that I was still there and that nothing was going to prevent that.

Christina and Hannah were out and about, so this gave me the house to myself. I placed all of our dogs outside in the yard so the house would be whisper quiet. I took my laptop and placed it on the dining room table with the onboard camera recording. That camera covered the dining room, the living room where a small stand with an old lamp by the fireplace was, and the door to Norman's old room.

After spending some time digging around, I found a large, gold Christian cross on a necklace. Considering the religion-laced incidents with Norman in the past, I figured he might not be too keen on seeing a cross again. I was hoping this would spark a better success rate than the already-great sessions we had seen so far.

It was early afternoon, so I kept all of the lights off. But I did light a few candles and place them on a coffee table in the living room. I had with me an old electromagnetic field tester, or more commonly referred to as an EMF detector. This would help me monitor any fluctuations in electromagnetic fields. High electromagnetic fields are believed to be very common in the presence of a spirit.

Armed with a cross, camera, and EMF detector, I sat down at the dining room table to attempt communication with the entity. The time was one in the afternoon.

I placed the cross at the edge of the table alongside the EMF detector. Of course, Norman was present, sitting firmly on the table I was at.

With the laptop camera rolling, I started to speak. The first thing I asked was if there was anybody there with me. Instantly, I heard a faint scratching sound come from the master bedroom. I leaned over in my chair to where I could see into the bedroom. I asked that if the spirit was the one making the scratching sound, could they do it again. Right on cue, the scratching sound occurred one more time. This time, however, the sound was much louder and reminded me of somebody taking their fingernails and dragging them down a wall.

I was honestly feeling a bit creeped out at that moment. For some reason, I was not feeling anything positive. Norman was beside me on the table, yet the undetermined sounds were coming from across the house. The air around me became heavy, and it was difficult to breathe. The air wasn't hot, but it had the same effect on my breathing.

When it's hot it is harder to breathe, and the air feels thick. There wasn't a temperature change at the moment, but the air had become very heavy. Knowing at this point that I was speaking to a spirit, I asked for it, or him, to come closer to the dining room table. I pointed out the EMF meter and explained that the closer he or she came, the higher the number would go and the faster the lights would flash.

This would tell me the spirit was right beside me. I asked to be approached, and the EMF lit up like a police car. The lights were flashing extremely rapidly, and the needle on the meter was buried past the highest level allotted for that device.

I then picked up the gold cross and dangled it in front of the table. The EMF meter immediately dropped back down to zero like nothing was there. I placed the cross back on the table and the meter maxed out again. I went back and forth with this routine. I would move the cross off the table, and then I would put it back. Each and every time, the meter would stop and start just like it did the first time.

It was evident at this point the entity was not very fond of that cross. This further validated all of the occurrences I documented in the past with Norman when religion was brought into the mix. It was also terrifying to realize that the spirit had that much energy right from the start. The reads I was documenting are not very common.

That was very intimidating.

With that in mind, I asked the entity if they were angry about something. Immediately, the master bedroom door shut and latched. The atmosphere around me became very still. I stood up and walked over to the bedroom door and reopened it. I then sat back down at the table. I apparently had struck a nerve with my line of questioning. Norman was angry about something, and he had just confirmed that.

Proceeding with that line of communication, I asked if the entity wished for me to leave, and without hesitation, a metallic scraping sound shot out of the master bedroom. This sounded like somebody dragging a metal bucket very slowly and lightly. I leaned over in my chair again to view the master bedroom. What happened next about gave me a heart attack, and the video would later show that.

I started to stand up. My intentions were to walk back over to my bedroom door. I took one step in that direction when the loudest, most disturbing animalistic hiss caught me by such surprise, that I literally stumbled backward into the wall and smacked my hand against my chest.

My heart was pounding so hard that I thought I was going to have medical issues. I stood there clenching my chest and composing myself.

I said out loud, in a nervous fashion, that it was fine, and I would sit back down. I did.

At that moment, beyond a shadow of a doubt, I knew that whatever was in my house was more than just your average spirit. This entity was very dark, angry, strong, and not afraid to intimidate. Believe me when I say it was daunting.

I sat at the table in silence for a few minutes before starting my line of questioning again.

One more time, I prompted the spirit to approach the table, and just like before, the EMF detector gave me a light show. Knowing that I had to take this further for my own peace of mind, I decided to test the spirit's tolerance. The entity obviously did not like the fact we were sharing the home, so I used that to fuel the uncanny events that happened next.

I stopped asking questions and decided to make a simple statement. In a confident and stern fashion, I told the spirit that this was my house and we play by my rules. I was barely finished with that sentence when the old lamp on the little stand directly to my right powered on, shook, and flickered sporadically like a malfunctioning strobe light at a disco.

Of course, I jerked quickly to look in that direction, nearly separating my head from my neck. I sat there dumbfounded. Apparently, the entity did not appreciate my choice of words.

I leaned back in my chair and started to breathe in and out very slowly. This was certainly a lot to take in. The activity in my home was very abundant and more than I had seen at a location in many years. The haunting part about all of it was the fact that this activity was always there, hiding behind a veil, just waiting to come out.

Norman could be doing this at any time, yet he waits until I prepare for it and prompt him to show himself. It reminded me all too well of darker times and past investigations that led to malevolent behavior and colleagues getting hurt.

Thoughts in my mind danced around each other as I considered all of his dangerous behavior before.

While I was sitting still in the chair, the air surrounding me became bitterly cold. The temperature drop was undoubtedly noticeable, and it sent shivers down my spine. I would later discover that the cold temperature was accompanied by something else.

It is one thing to witness spiritual activity firsthand and in real time. It is another for something to be happening and you have no clue it's even going on. When you later learn that something was right there, so close, and you were oblivious to it, well my friends, that is the scariest feeling of them all. It is downright unsettling.

I would later discover from the laptop's camera footage that supernatural activity was literally occurring directly behind me. After the excitement of the lamp situation, I decided to take a break, for the better of all parties involved, and review everything that had been documented.

I started the video over and began watching my entire communication session. Where I was sitting, in the recording, you can see the door to Norman's old room, as I stated before. I was staring off into the living room when that bedroom door cracked open ever so slightly. It continued to open at such a remarkably slow and patient pace that watching the video literally gave me cold chills.

Up until then, all that ever happened with a door was it closing on it's own, and that was the one to the master bedroom. This was much different. This was another door, coincidentally Norman's door, and this time it was opening. This was incredible to realize. To turn a doorknob and push or pull open a door takes force. I was left speechless realizing the strength he had and the amount of energy this spirit must be able to influence.

This happened right behind me while experiencing the extreme temperature drop.

As I watched the footage over and over, I kept feeling as if something was in the darkness of that room peering out and just staring right through me. I certainly can't validate that, but that was the feeling I had.

I watched the video a few more times before shutting down the laptop to collect myself. I was feeling very exhausted, dizzy, empty, and a little disoriented. My communication session lasted about an hour and a half. That was a lot of great footage and experiences to have gained and document in such a short amount of time.

Yet none of it provided any solid answers to our ongoing questions about Norman.

Christina returned home, and I briefed her on everything that had happened while she was gone. She watched the video, and I could literally see the cold chills take over her body when she saw that door slowly open without human intervention. We both agreed to take a break from Norman and our personal paranormal case for a while. That is, if he would let us.

I knew of a perfect place to take him. Since the spring, Christina and I had been building a cabin for ourselves with the intent of eventually moving into it permanently upon completion. So I packed Norman away in his suitcase and took him there.

Inside, I kept him locked in his suitcase and stored up in one of the lofts. There wasn't any power to the building yet, so he was being stored in a dead spot. There wouldn't be a lot for him to pull energy from unless a massive storm were to come through.

I wasn't too concerned at that point that he would be able to accomplish anything of relevance. I especially wasn't worried that he would be affecting us back home. It was one thing to have him sitting in front of you and cause something to happen from across the house—he was at least in the same general vicinity. But at the cabin, he would be locked away, miles away from anyone—most importantly, us. He was out of sight and out of mind for the next few weeks while we attempted to get back to a somewhat normal life.

Upon returning back home, the place felt lighter. It seemed less dark, figuratively speaking. I think a huge weight had been lifted from our shoulders. We believed it was a wise decision to isolate him further from us. This would give us the time we needed to hopefully come up with a remedy that solved all.

We took the problem out of the equation, but things still weren't adding up. Norman was a patient entity. He would wait for the opportune time to strike again. But this time, for me, he would go too far.

13

The Next Step

Up until this point, all of Norman's violent, human-based attacks were directed toward me. Three years of walking on eggshells around a haunted doll we were guilty of welcoming into our home.

History had taught me that Norman does not like male figures. So it was never a concern of ours that Christina and Hannah would ever find themselves on the receiving end of a Norman fit.

Christina and Hannah certainly had their fill from the haunted department. But Christina was about to feel the wrath of Norman, and I believe he intended to get at me through her. It is like when a kidnapper holds a person hostage for leverage. They are doing it to gain something in trade from somebody else. I think Norman resorted to going beyond his typical attacks and went straight for what mattered the most to me. The thing that matters the most to me is my wife, Christina.

That day in August was more alarming to me than any time in the past I had been hospitalized. As frightening as those times were, the reality of my wife getting hurt completely dwarfed any concerns I had for myself.

Christina and I left our house that day to continue work on our cabin. We had not made any more progress on the cabin since we locked Norman away in there, so we were a little behind in our construction. But it was nice to have a quiet and safe home while Norman was gone. We definitely had missed that normal feeling.

That day, we had planned to begin work on adding electricity to the building. Before we could put up any sheet rock on the walls, the electrical outlets and wires needed to be run throughout. I had the main structure with a door and windows and a set of stairs, but nothing else had been completed yet.

We arrived at the cabin around lunchtime that day.

The first thing I did was go up to the loft I had stored Norman in. I wanted to check and see if anything was out of place. Everything was fine and just how I had left it. All that was in the building were boxes we had stored there from the house and some construction supplies.

Christina and I knew he would be returning home with us that day once we left. We had talked a great deal on the way to the cabin about ridding ourselves of him. We were still unsure as to what to do with him, but our focus on that would meet a roadblock soon enough.

There were two lofts in the cabin. One had steps to it while the other did not. Christina was working at the top of the loft with steps, sweeping construction debris. I was on the first floor moving boxes around and measuring cable to run through the cabin.

I glanced over at the suitcase Norman was in. I had placed it on a table we had brought in. I guess curiosity got the better of me. I had yet to actually look inside to make sure the doll was even still in there. It's silly to think that somehow the doll could manage to open the case from the inside and get out. But nothing was really beyond the realm of believability at that point concerning him. I stopped what I was doing and walked over to the table where he was resting.

I grabbed the case and unlatched both locks. As soon as I opened the case, I heard a loud and heavy tumble of sorts from around the corner from where I was standing. It sounded like a sack of potatoes had plummeted to the floor. Whatever hit the floor had enough force to cause a vibration that I could feel.

Norman was still in his case, resting exactly how I had left him. You would think I would be used to it by now, but that little, minacious grin spoke words without saying a thing. As I glanced at him, I just knew I was about to find something bad around that corner of the cabin.

I yelled out to Christina and asked her if she heard that sound and what was it. She never responded. I yelled her name again. Nothing but silence surrounded the cabin. In a panic, I closed up his case and ran around the corner to see what, exactly, made the loud boom.

I almost vomited when I rounded the corner to see Christina laying on the floor. She was flat on her back and unconscious. You can imagine that my first thoughts were not good. I honestly thought I came around that corner to find her dead. She was lifeless.

As I quickly approached her, I noticed her chest moving up and down ever so softly. She was still alive. I knelt down beside her and started saying her name over and over again. I glanced around the area, looking for blood or anything to help me figure out the severity of the situation.

I looked up the stairs as she was laying at the bottom. I had no choice but to believe she had fallen down them. I saw nothing immediately that would have explained her fall, and she wasn't speaking to help me out in that department. A few moments passed, and her eyes slowly began to open. She was disoriented.

I placed my arms underneath her shoulders to help lift her up. She immediately screamed in total agony. Something was seriously wrong. Christina asked me what had just happened, and I had no idea. I told her I was in the other room looking in on Norman when I heard the fall.

She could not move, and I was worried she had hurt something terribly. Awful thoughts raced through my brain as I feared she was paralyzed.

Christina was in tears. I can count on one hand the times in over ten years I had ever seen her cry. It takes a lot to bring her to tears. She was in some serious pain as she complained to me about her lower back and asked me to call for help. That was a bold statement from Christina. She never asks for help. She is always tough as nails to a fault. I knew by her asking me to call for help that she must have believed herself to be seriously hurt.

I made the call to 911 emergency services.

After about fifteen minutes, the ambulance arrived. She was taken to New Hanover Regional Medical Center in Wilmington, North Carolina. I followed along behind her, biting at the bit to find out if she was going to be alright or if this accident was going to cause more-permanent damage.

I also heavily pondered the idea that what happened was not an accident. What were the chances of her falling down that flight of steps at the exact moment I opened up the case to reveal Norman? I was thinking all sorts of crazy things. What if Christina falling was the doll seeking revenge?

Upon arrival, they immediately took her back through the emergency room. The staff wasted no time ordering up and carrying out a CAT scan, x-rays, and other tests to determine the severity of her fall.

After a few hours, all of the tests came back normal. Luckily for us, she did not have any broken bones or permanent damage. She did, however, have a torn muscle in her lower back.

Just like the times before that involved me, the doctor could not find anything seriously wrong with Christina. She was ordered by the doctor to stay in bed until it healed. Frankly, she had no choice. The pain was so excruciating, she could barely move. Christina described it to me like getting stabbed in the back with a butcher knife every time she attempted to move.

The nurses and doctor monitored her for a few more hours before finally discharging her.

On the way home, she and I discussed in better detail what had taken place at the cabin. This wasn't a conversation we were going to have at the hospital considering all of the eyes and ears around us. Now, with a clear head and all of the excitement over, Christina could finally confide those moments before she took a dive down the stairs in the cabin.

She told me she had been sweeping at the top of the steps, cleaning up sawdust. She had stopped for a moment to look down the stairs and around our cabin. Christina said she was daydreaming about how it was all going to look when it was said and done.

Then she felt as if she wasn't alone up in the loft. She had an overwhelming feeling come over her. It was that feeling you get when you just know somebody is standing behind you. At first, she thought that I had somehow snuck up the steps and was about to pull a prank on her. Christina turned around, expecting to catch me in mid-prank. Instead, she said the entire room went black and she passed out. The next thing she remembered was me crouched down over top of her screaming her name.

I couldn't help but be reminded of when I blacked out and woke up to being rushed to the hospital. This was all too real and all too familiar to us.

I looked at her as we approached our house and asked if she was thinking the same thing I was.

Christina did not have to really say it. I knew she was thinking that doll shoved her down the steps in some way. Certainly there were other, more believable reasons she could have fallen, but nothing was going to change our minds. Her blackout was unexplained at the hospital, and the only advice given was to keep an eye on it. How the hell do you keep an eye on blacking out? I never did understand that one.

The intrigue and excitement concerning Norman was now gone between the both of us. There was no limitation to him anymore. I don't think there ever really was. Here we were again, victims of yet another one of his dangerous schemes. It was evident that whatever was residing in Norman was spiteful, hateful, and seeking out some sort of revenge. He is methodical, intelligent and very aware of his surroundings. I have never witnessed such a powerful and dark spirit before.

As we drove, I told Christina how bad I felt about the entire thing. My stomach had been in knots. The thought of losing her killed me a little inside. I felt impotent. There was nothing I could do for Christina. Only time was going to heal her wounds. And I'm not certain that some psychological wounds can even be healed.

So now Norman was going after more than just me, and that certainly changed the way I thought about our ongoing research with him. Something was going to have to change. When was enough going to be enough?

Sure, we started this with the betterment of paranormal research in mind. I mean, who wouldn't if they were in our place? We as researchers work hard every day for years on end just for a glimpse into the afterlife. When the afterlife crash-lands smack dab in the middle of your own home, you can't help but be grateful for a moment. But all things come to an end eventually. We started this curious and with sincere intentions. But the years of torment have weighed heavy on us.

That night, I made Christina as comfortable as possible in our bed. But the strangeness that came with Norman wasn't done coming.

Christina and I were both on the bed relaxing and watching television. The room was dark, and everything had appeared to calm down for the night. The illumination from the television was the only light in the room. Everything was composed and reposeful for the most part, considering the great amount of pain she was in. Typically, when Norman acts out on a grand scale, there is breathing room left afterward. But this time he wanted to be sure we knew he was still waiting and watching. It's like he wanted to whisper to us, "I'm always here."

The really crazy thing was the fact that Norman was nowhere even close by. Having been caught up in all of the excitement of Christina's fall and the hospital, we never did return to the cabin for Norman. He was still there. If anything was a testament to his control, reach, and power, it was what happened next.

We were watching television when Christina jerked her leg in a panicked fashion. Of course, my attention went immediately to her. At first, I thought maybe it was just a twitch or something related to her fall, but it wasn't. Christina had a really surprised look on her face. She looked at me and said something just tickled her foot.

Logical thinking came over me at that moment. Our dogs are always rubbing themselves on us, so that was naturally my first thought. Or maybe I just didn't want to believe it was Norman. He wasn't around, so he was out of sight and out of mind. I jumped up from the bed to take a look around the room, thinking that maybe one of our dogs brushed up against her foot.

There was nothing. All of the dogs were lying out in the living room, asleep. Christina and I were the only living things in the bedroom. We both knew that Norman was miles away, locked up in the cabin, but was he really miles away?

Christina was authentically spooked. She told me that the tickle felt exactly like somebody taking a single finger and slowly brushing it down the bottom of her foot. I kept looking around the room, and there simply wasn't anything to have justified the cause. I even asked Christina if it were possible that an insect could have landed on her foot. She said no. The feeling of an insect is undeniable; this was something else. Christina and I both knew that something paranormal had been the cause. I think at this point, we were just hoping for something normal to be to blame.

I walked into our bathroom while Christina remained on the bed. There's no real way to put it other than I had to urinate. But I have to tell you that because that is what I was doing when the next fantastical occurrence took place. Somehow, Norman was still able to affect us. He was still able to haunt our house without even being present.

I was in the middle of using the bathroom when all of a sudden, from behind me, I felt my shirt being pulled. I instantly stopped urinating and turned around, completely expecting either Christina to be standing there or one of the dogs.

You can think about a lot in just a second. The pull on my shirt was so real and so convincing, that in my mind, I just knew it had to be something of flesh and blood doing it. I was wrong. I yelled out, "What in the world?"

Christina asked what I was going on about, and I told her. She was still firmly on the bed and no dogs had come out of our living room and into the bedroom. I was alone in that bathroom when something pulled down on the lower part of my shirt. Everybody knows that feeling when a person tugs on your clothing. This felt exactly like that.

Considering the nature of the pull, I believed a young child or a dog was the culprit. No young children were there, so it just had to be one of our dogs.

Like I said, I expected to turn around and see at least Tank tugging on me with his mouth because he needed to go outside or something. This just wasn't the case. Within ten minutes of each other, Christina had been tickled and I had my shirt tugged by something we could not see or find. This was incredible.

Sure, we have witnessed objects moving, been the victims of physical attacks, and seen Norman do things that defy physics. But, when something subtle happens behind a mask of playfulness, a new level of fear arises. I think it is scarier to know that he could have done harm but instead didn't. It was almost as if the spirit inside of Norman was saying, "You know what I am capable of, so here's a little reminder that what just happened could have been entirely worse."

The rest of the night went without incident but did not go without heavy pondering about the entire situation. I firmly believed that all of our time spent around Norman led to more of that spiritual magnetism I talked about before. But how long could it last? His actions were just another reason to believe he had no boundaries or very little limitations across the spiritual realm. He wasn't confined to that doll, and that has to be the scariest part about the whole situation.

That train of thought made me think all the way back to when we first came into contact with him at that antique shop. His box had very visible scratch marks on it as if something was trying to get out. Inside, very bizarre rhymes were written in different handwriting alluding to his origin and intent. Was Norman actually happy in his locked box, or was he just waiting to be broken free so havoc could be wreaked? It was like Pandora had built that box herself and placed everything horrific inside the heart of that doll. We opened it and we got what we asked for—and then some.

Christina and I both agreed that we would no longer be taking one for the team so to speak. Three years' worth of research into one of the most haunted objects I had ever seen was going to come to an end. Christina was also more than frustrated. If Norman's attacks were now extending to more of the family, what would be next? How far could we possibly let this go before something irreversible happened? Christina agreed with me that it was time to get rid of the doll. We both agreed that it was time to move on from this chapter in our lives. We could not live like this anymore, and I was not going to stand for my wife to be in the direct line of danger.

Over the next week, Christina did exactly what the doctor ordered. She stayed in bed while I took care of her hand and foot. She bounced back, and we started to move on.

14

The Numbers Don't Lie

Before I made a final decision on what to do with Norman, I wanted some closing test results just to finalize the file on his case. It had been a while since I simply took some notes on his bizarre ability to affect surrounding temperatures and electromagnetic energies.

When I ran tests in the past, Norman demonstrated temperature drops and extremely high reads on the electromagnetic field tester. For a doll that wasn't mechanical in any way, that was quite astonishing. I figured for curiosity's sake and documentation purposes I would conduct follow-up tests on the haunted doll just to bring everything full circle.

In early September, I decided to spend a day experimenting with Norman in various situations and atmospheres. I figured the best place to start was at our cabin.

There wasn't any power or temperature control, so anything beyond the norm during testing would certainly stand out. That was also the last place where we had known, severe activity with him. The foot tickling and my shirt being tugged paled in comparison to what happened at the cabin. There, he struck, and he struck hard.

For a place with no power, he most definitely displayed a seemingly endless energy source. I brought his old rocking chair with me in hopes of sparking something familiar within him. This was the same rocking chair he sat content in for a long time in his own room.

When I arrived at the cabin, I wasted no time getting started. I was there to do one job and one job only. I wanted to document his current status. The last interaction we had with him that we knew of was Christina's fall down the stairs.

I placed the rocking chair inside and took Norman from his case. I sat Norman in the chair. I was running both night vision and standard vision cameras.

The heat index outside was one hundred and five degrees. It should have been unbearable in the building, but upon entering, I had immediately noticed the difference in the temperature inside versus the outside. There was at least a twenty-five-degree variance, with the interior being much cooler. Considering it was the middle of the day, this was unheard of. It should have felt like an oven on the inside with a temperature of at least one hundred degrees.

However, on average, the interior of the cabin was reading around seventy-four degrees throughout.

I squatted down and aimed my temperature gun at the rocking chair Norman was sitting in to document a baseline temperature. The temperature was rocking back and forth between seventy-four and seventy-five degrees Fahrenheit. Although that was odd, and it should have been much hotter inside, it still wasn't anything to chalk up to paranormal activity.

Before I could even write down the temperature I had just physically documented, the door to the cabin whipped open with great force. It was like a storm had just dropped right outside the door, yet it was clear as day. I obviously jumped from my squatting position. The door crashing open was enough to get my blood pumping. It appeared that Norman was wasting no time showing me he was still in control. There wasn't any breathing room here. He went right for it. No buildup. No nothing.

I ran over to the door just to make sure nobody was outside. Not that there would be anyway. The cabin was far off the beaten path. I shut the door and returned to the rocking chair to continue documenting Norman.

This time when I aimed the temperature gun at him, the temperature surrounding him had dropped over ten degrees. This was definitely something to take note of. Barely sixty seconds had passed since I first logged the temperature and the door flew open. Ten degrees in less than a minute was just uncanny. Temperature just doesn't drop that fast. There isn't a situation out there in which the temperature would drop at that speed. This was the beginning of September in North Carolina. It doesn't drop to sixty-three degrees in a building without temperature control.

As I was writing all of this down, my attention was taken by the sound of faint creaking. Back and forth and back and forth. It only took me a second to realize that the creaking sound was the rocking chair moving slightly back and forth. The movement was so subtle that if you were just walking by it, it would go unnoticed.

But my focus was now entirely on it, so I noticed.

At first, I wanted to believe that the door flying open caused the chair to start moving ever so slightly, but a few minutes had passed since then, and the chair had just started doing it.

Without hesitation, I grabbed an electromagnetic field tester to see if there was any unexplainable energy around Norman. At first, there wasn't a field of any kind. This is how he should always be. Norman is nothing but plastic and cloth. He does not take batteries, nor does he have any electrical components. For all intents and purposes, like any other inanimate toy, Norman should always register as a zero on the electromagnetic field tester.

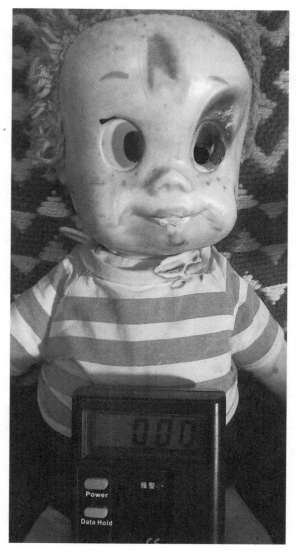

Normal EMF reading

But it wasn't long before my zero turned into numbers of concern. In the center of his chest, he immediately caused a forty-three-point spike on the meter. A surge of great proportions must have taken place for the numbers on the gauge to leap like that.

If that wasn't enough, within just a second, the field tester jumped to an eighty-seven. The center of his chest seemed to be the hot spot and source of energy for the reads.

As if eighty-seven wasn't a high enough number to brag about, the meter beeped and jumped to a staggering 141. I had never in my life seen an inanimate, nonelectrical object display such high reads. The only explanation fell within the realm of the paranormal, and it fell there very comfortably, without argument.

Norman was displaying his own energy source, which could only be explained as spiritual energy.

These numbers were being registered on the Gauss scale of the meter. An electromagnetic field tester commonly has two modes for measurement, Gauss and Tesla. Tesla measures magnetic flux density while Gauss registers magnetic field strength. Both are scientifically accepted units for measuring magnetic fields; however, the more appropriate mode for paranormal research would be Gauss. The strength of the field is what helps us determine the power of the spirit.

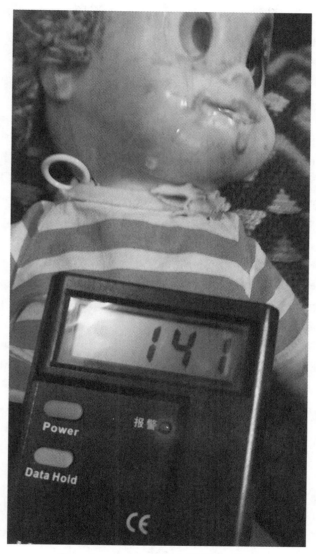

Very abnormal, very high EMF reading

These were numbers we would expect to see something like a refrigerator or microwave give off. Instead, these reads were being emitted from a plastic doll with no source of power. I had no choice but to believe that *he* was the source of power.

I sat on the floor next to him, just pondering the amazing documentation once again. Here I was, proving that the doll had measurable energy on his own. I cannot stress how important that is in the field of paranormal research. Over the years, Norman had displayed intelligence and power, and adding these results solidified just how haunted he really was.

Within thirty minutes of arriving at the cabin I had witnessed the door slam open, a crazy temperature drop around Norman, and extremely high electromagnetic fields surrounding the doll.

The truly scary thought was the fact that he was capable of all of this without any man-made, outside power source. I could only wonder what level he could achieve if given an ample supply of energy. This was a question that all-too-often rattled my brain. We witnessed it before within our home, and we witnessed it during Hurricane Matthew when the storm brought such high levels of ionic energy.

My testing once again proved that Norman had his own atmosphere. He effected any area he resided in. What more did a person need to prove they had a haunted doll? I was beyond validating it at this point. Hell, I think I was beyond that point well before this. It was like continuing to do tests to prove the sky was blue. We know it's blue. It isn't necessary to point out why anymore. Between all of the video and research we had, there was no denying our lives had been rattled by an evil and haunted doll.

This was the point where the angel appeared on one shoulder and the devil on the other. I can't believe I was thinking such things, but even after all that had happened, I was considering keeping him. Having something like Norman was a once-in-a-lifetime opportunity. It was especially a grand opportunity for the field of paranormal research. Some people work their whole lives in hopes of discovering something as powerful as the entity inside of Norman. They work hard hoping to prove that there is an existence beyond human life. With Norman, we had that.

Here I was, fighting myself and going against everything I believed by actually contemplating keeping him. But I talked myself out of it. I knew through all of my research I had everything I needed to prove his reality. I knew that in the end, this was a very drawn out personal experience for my family. The data and the stories were already there and set in stone. What more did I possibly need to happen?

It was a dark realization that day to see the data once again point to favoring Norman's ability. It was like I needed some sort of reassurance that Norman was in fact haunted. I couldn't believe I was even considering keeping him, but that was solely thanks to the lifelong paranormal researcher in me. Sometimes you just have to end the case yourself. I can't stress enough how hard of a decision that was to make.

On one hand, you might think that we should have just run from it years ago. On the other hand, you might agree that this was an amazing opportunity to further the field of paranormal research. Three years' worth of home field research on the haunted doll was going to have to be enough. It was time to move on.

Every time we attempted to rid ourselves of him in the past, he simply came right back. More extensive measures were going to have to be taken at this point.

Timing was everything, however, and we had an approaching storm to consider before any more real thought could be placed on the Norman situation. Norman was going to have one more golden opportunity to cause waves in our realm before I would be forced to take permanent action. I returned home to continue preparing with Christina for the upcoming hurricane.

15

Hurricane Dorian

It was the day before the hurricane was projected to hit us head on. Even though our focus should have been entirely on what Mother Nature had in store for us, Christina and I couldn't help but continue the conversation about Norman. We gave up the normal life a long time ago. Now we lived the Norman life.

We were at our house packing up supplies and preparing the place for the storm. We wanted to leave the house in the best shape we could for the sake of Hannah and her boyfriend. Tank and Duck, two of our dogs, accompanied us to the cabin while the rest stayed at the house with Hannah. We knew Norman would be at the cabin with us, and with that came a sense of relief as far as Hannah was concerned.

Hannah was going to man the house with her boy-friend during the storm. She was now eighteen, and parts of Christina and me were starting to shine through in her. We were proud to see her take shape as a strong woman, one capable of protecting her twenty-two-year-old boyfriend while he played video games. Yes, this kid wouldn't know survival if it hit him in the face. Thankfully for him, he was with somebody who does.

Although honestly, I think Hannah's motive was rooted in the fact we were leaving Norman at the cabin with us. She was an adult now, and it was her choice to face the storm at our house, but the last thing we were going to do was keep Norman there. And frankly, Hannah, at great length, kept reminding us of that fact.

At the same time, I reminded Christina how Norman had been able to affect things even when he wasn't around. That had us both worried to a degree. If something were to happen at our house during the hurricane, Hannah would be trapped and stuck fending for herself. There wouldn't be a thing we could do to stop it or even prevent it. We would be dealing with our own problems at the cabin concerning the storm.

We both figured him being trapped with us would solve the problem and keep his mind off of anything else. However, I couldn't help but think back to the situation at the hotel when he predicted things that eventually happened.

Worse yet, he caused issues with Darren's plane, and he wasn't even remotely close to him.

It honestly seemed that anybody who came into contact with Norman left with a connection, and that connection opened up a line between them and him. From what we had seen so far, I couldn't help but subscribe to that idea.

But I couldn't focus on that at the moment.

Christina was packing up the normal stuff. Clothes and other necessities were her priority while mine were cameras and paranormal research equipment. Before the storm was to arrive, I was taking full advantage of still having electrical power to the house. So believe me when I tell you that just about every outlet in the house was being used by some piece of equipment.

I fully expected Norman to be active during the hurricane. He has haunted every place he's been and even places he has not. I honestly would have been slightly disappointed if our stay at the cabin was uneventful. So I wasn't going to that cabin without everything I had to document Norman if he were to act up again.

Part of me knew that this was going to be the last time we ever had the opportunity to document our haunted doll. Christina and I both knew that after the hurricane we would be disposing of him in some way. We just had yet to figure that one out. Needless to say, I was hoping for the best in paranormal activity at the cabin.

Considering his patterns and everything I had documented over the past three years, everything was going to be perfectly in place for him to do so. We had the huge storm to count on with all of that natural ionic energy. We would be isolated and impotent in many ways. That is something Norman has demonstrated liking. He likes having the upper hand. So all of the elements were going to be there. He was going to have us right where he wanted us, and we would have no choice but to live it—and hopefully live through it.

Hannah and her boyfriend were just as busy preparing, while also avoiding any conversation involving the doll. Hannah had been very gun shy about the hurricane. She had heard from us what had happened during hurricane Matthew involving Norman. So she had every right to be concerned. That was a landmark night as far as witnessing the most extreme activity from the haunted doll.

We were in a tough situation with a lot to talk about and consider. The family was planning on separating during the storm so we could keep Norman as far away from Hannah as possible. So that meant if something happened to Hannah we wouldn't know, let alone be able to even get to her. That worked the other way as well. If something happened to us at the cabin, she wouldn't even know.

Norman would be more apt to come at me and Christina than he would Hannah, but we were not going to take any chances. Although in the past he did give her a run for her money a few times, he never threatened physical harm. I think Hannah reminded Norman of the girl that once owned him.

My forty-second birthday was closing in and so was the hurricane. I have to say "Dorian" was probably the best name for a storm in history. At least it means, "child of the sea." Like hurricane Matthew years prior, our guard was up, cameras were ready, and gear was locked and loaded.

Christina and I live for this stuff. We are survivalists, and any time the grid of society is going to be shut down, we run right at the opportunity. We took a huge risk using our cabin as shelter. Our only power would be supplied by a short-lived generator.

Living conditions were not going to be in our favor. We would be using sleeping bags and pretty much anything else you would expect while camping. The only difference between staying in the cabin and out in the wilderness was the security of four walls and a roof.

Christina and I settled into the cabin for the night, awaiting Hurricane Dorian's arrival. We had the whole night ahead of us as far as Norman was concerned, so we wasted no time setting up to see just how far we could push him. That sounds a little unstable on our part, but for me, this would act as the final documented haunt of his. If nothing happened, nothing happened. But we had to try before I officially said goodbye. In retrospect, I am certainly glad we tried, because what happened that night gave me one hefty and last contribution to the Norman case file.

It had been gloomy all day with the approaching storm, so light inside the cabin was already going to be an issue. We did have our little generator and a handful of flashlights. I had hooked up a single lamp inside the cabin. Our generator was small and could only power a few devices. We were lucky to get a fan, a light, and our phone chargers out of it.

After settling in, we decided to go ahead and start filming a session with Norman. It was about ten in the evening when we actually sat down in front of him to conduct work. Like before, I placed Norman back in his rocking chair, so he was the center of attention for the night. Outside, the wind and rain were starting to pick up beyond a typical storm. We knew it wouldn't be long before Hurricane Dorian was upon us.

I wish I could say more, but for the first few hours of attempting communication with Norman, nothing happened. It was very quiet. The calmness inside the cabin was unsettling. Outside, we could hear the wind whipping and the elements battering the sides of the cabin, but inside seemed like an entirely different world.

Norman in his chair at the cabin

Norman sat quietly in his rocking chair while we made attempt after attempt to get him to do something. For nearly three hours, Norman just sat there, content and quiet. We had nothing else to do, so we continued trying to get Norman to interact with us.

At about one thirty in the morning, the rain was becoming so intense outside, Christina and I could barely hear one another talking. We knew that anything audible captured during those sessions would have to be ruled out. Part of me believed that was why Norman was staying so quiet. What would have been the point?

All we could hear was debris hitting the sides of the cabin and the wind racing along the roof of the building. The rain pounded the roof harder than I think I have ever heard it do so. On top of all of that, the running sound of the generator left no room to decipher any sort of sound inside.

It was loud all around us.

It was scary to hear all of that going on outside, especially when we couldn't see anything through the windows. It was pitch black. You could not see a foot in front of you. Even when I shined a flashlight through the window, all I could see was a wall of water pouring from the sky.

Two in the morning arrived, and I decided to listen back to my camera. I was going to review our communication session so far and hopefully discover something out of the ordinary we did not notice at the time. Luckily for us, we did capture a disembodied voice on my camera.

At the time of the communication session, Christina was asking Norman how he felt about us planning to get rid of him. To our own ears, we heard nothing at the time. But after plugging my headphones into the camera and reviewing that section, we could hear a voice plain as day.

The voice softly said, "You can't."

Now this is something we had heard Norman say numerous times across a handful of communication sessions, but this time, his response seemed to be more in tune to the question. All of this talk about getting rid of him, and he was answering up. I took it as a threat to be honest.

He knew in the past we had tried to get rid of him and were unsuccessful. I think he was furthering his confidence by telling us, once again, that we couldn't get rid of him even if we tried. Capturing that voice sparked excitement within Christina and me. For hours, we had thought Norman was going to remain stagnant in the paranormal activity department. But here he was, responding to us all along.

I played that part of the video over and over, and that was the only thing said at that moment. I put the camera down and grabbed my cell phone to check the status on the hurricane. I had been following along with the Doppler radar all evening.

That's when it happened. And when I say it happened, it happened all at once, very fast, and completely chaotically.

Our generator outside started sputtering like it was running out of gas. The one lamp I had lighting up the interior of the cabin started to flicker. Christina was sitting right next to me on the floor as we continued to face Norman in his chair. She said, "Here we go."

We were right in the middle of the peak of Hurricane Dorian.

Within a few seconds, our entire cabin was dark. The generator powered off, and there we were, caught inside with no visibility at the moment other than the light from my cell phone. We scrambled around looking for our flashlights.

The light from my cell phone made it very disorienting inside as it frantically bounced off of the walls while we raced to find more lighting. I shouted out to Christina so she could hear me over the pouring rain. I said, "Listen, Christina!"

I had heard movement from within the cabin. Something was moving inside with us. We both stopped and stood very still in the dark.

I could hear Norman's rocking chair slowly moving back and forward. Neither one of us had been near it to have hit it or bumped it during the chaos.

I started snapping pictures in Norman's general direction so I would at least have the flash from the cell phone's camera lighting up the room. I could not shoot video because I didn't have a light source, but I could take pictures one at a time. Using my cell phone was the only option considering how fast things were taking place. There just wasn't time to stop, find a camera, and start recording from it.

Norman was now in a standing position. I grabbed a hold of Christina and showed her the picture I had just seen. As I was taking the pictures, I saw his image in real time standing in the rocking chair. I showed Christina, and all she could say, in a very confused fashion, was, "How is he standing up now?"

The peak of the storm was outside, and now the peak of Norman was happening inside. I started snapping more pictures in his direction. One right after another. Each and every time, the flash would light up the cabin. He was gone.

Norman standing in the rocking chair on his own

But was he? No longer was he standing on the rocking chair. The chair itself was violently rocking back and forth at this point. I could feel Christina gripping my arm as we could hear nothing but the sound of the rocking chair and the horrible weather beating on the cabin.

Unexplained anomaly, and Norman is missing

I snapped more and more pictures in an attempt to use the flash to locate Norman. I snapped photographs in every direction, side to side and up and down. Sure, I could have just turned on the flashlight on the cell phone, but that would have prevented me from taking pictures. My phone did not allow the flashlight to be implemented while using the camera feature.

At that moment, I had to think fast, and doing what little I could to document had to happen because something very big was taking place.

The pictures revealed something moving from the rocking chair to the ceiling. It was blurry like the image at Big Steve's house and looked very similar in design. Once again it appeared sandy and gritty. But it wasn't blurry because I was moving the cell phone too fast. If you focus on everything else in the room, all of it is in focus. Only the anomaly appears that way, and that had to be due to its amazing speed.

The anomaly is moving quickly, and Norman is still missing

In the images, you can see that Norman is no longer in the rocking chair. You can also see a strange anomaly shoot from that chair to beyond the loft above. The velocity of movement had to have been great considering I was taking single pictures standing still, and the captured image still looked to be moving at high speed. It had to be Norman.

You could see that whatever was pictured had mass to it. In the images you can clearly see the majority of the cabin's interior. I had no choice but to believe that what I captured was him moving to wherever he ended up. But where could he have gone?

Then I took the picture that ended it all. I was aiming my cell phone upward to the ceiling when I snapped one of the most disturbing pictures in my career. There was Norman, hanging from the ceiling.

Norman located hanging from the cabin's ceiling

Although the picture isn't high definition or crystal clear, there was no denying that there was Norman, hanging from the ceiling. I saw him with my own two eyes when the flash went off. To this day, I cannot look at that picture without the coldest of chills running down my back. There is just something beyond creepy to it.

To know this was happening around us as we feared for ourselves in the dark wasn't an easy thing to swallow. It makes me think back to all of the other times we witnessed something or captured something phenomenal on video or in an image. It also makes me think of all the times we didn't. Just like the old man I saw walk into Norman's room, I wondered how many times these things were happening all around us and we had no clue. To me, that makes the situation even more frightening.

I immediately started taking more pictures in hopes of documenting even more movement.

Instead, I found Norman on the floor just a few feet from where Christina and I were standing. We did not hear him drop.

Norman fell back to the floor

A few moments after I documented Norman on the floor, our generator turned back on and we had visibility inside once again. When the generator had turned off initially, I thought it had simply run out of gas at the wrong time. I have never witnessed a generator power back on by itself. This is the type of generator with a cord you have to pull and pull with force to crank it up. Norman had made that generator turn off, and I couldn't be convinced otherwise.

The picture of Norman fourteen feet in the air, dangling from the ceiling, has got to be the best image I have ever taken in my life for the field of paranormal research. Hell, it would take a ladder to reach that area, and Norman just made it happen on his own.

One minute he was sitting in the rocking chair, the next minute he was standing, and then the next he was above us in an unreachable location. That blackout was the craziest thirty seconds of my life. A lot had taken place—and, even stranger, been documented from a single cell phone. I felt excited and emotionally disturbed at the same time. Witnessing something so unbelievable right before your eyes leaves one nearly speechless.

I have captured a lot of questionable and intriguing images and video over the past twenty-some years, but there was just something to that photograph that stood above the rest. All of those urban legends, folk tales, and ghost stories about haunted dolls I had heard over the years didn't hold a candle to seeing and living the real thing.

We were right to have conducted that communication session during the hurricane. And that storm certainly brought enough ionic energy to give Norman what he needed to manifest beyond an inanimate doll.

Christina and I had seen it with our own two eyes and had the photographs to prove it all. This was proof that Norman could control and manipulate the toy shell.

Over the years, we had documented Norman turning his head and moving it in ways that the toy wasn't even designed to do. Over the years, we had caught glimpses of him moving throughout the house. But this was the first time that we were standing right there in the same room with him moving right above us. Christina and I both felt even more intimidated by our haunted doll. It is easy to think you have seen it all when in reality you have only scratched the surface.

The storm was all over. The night with Norman was all over. The next morning, I was scrolling through my phone and found an image that I did not take. Well, at least I don't remember taking it. Considering all that happened and how fast it did, it was very possible I did. However, I was never that close to Norman when the power went out.

The picture was immediately noticeable and very out of place. As if the image wasn't bizarre enough to begin with, the lack of lighting and overall ambience was baffling. You have to look really close, but in the bottom left of the image you can see Norman's face, as if he took the picture himself. As silly as that sounds, that is the only way I can truly describe it. I assure you he is there in that image.

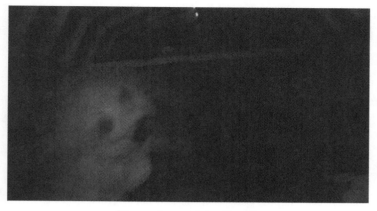

Norman's unexplainable selfie

I'm not certain at what time this photograph would have been taken, but it fell after all of the blackout photos in the camera roll. So sometime after Norman stood up in the rocking chair and moved around the room, this picture was captured. It makes me uneasy to think that maybe I did snap that picture and maybe he was that close to me at the time, and I just didn't realize it. But when I was taking pictures, the flash was being used. This picture clearly shows that no flash was being used.

The storm was gone and our final night with Norman was over. Once again, it would take a hurricane to bring out a true display of this entity's capabilities. But, like clockwork, we had to face the outcome of the storm. Damage, flooding, no power, and basically being trapped at our cabin until the city could revive itself.

I spent my forty-second birthday standing on my cabin's porch, feeling like I was on a boat. I had a lot of time to ponder during that time.

Christina and I agreed to move into the cabin on a more permanent basis just to keep Norman away from everyone and everything else. We could keep a safer eye on him there. This kept him out of our house and away from Hannah. That was part of a solution to the problem, but it didn't solve it entirely.

I felt I had enough to finally close the case file on Norman the haunted doll. I felt like I had a monkey on my back with an important decision to make. There was one big question still looming in the air. What do I do with Norman?

16

Where I Stand

I felt at this point I just needed to come to terms with what Norman was and quit fighting ages of habitual actions and decades of a one-track mind. It was time to be more open-minded and stop keeping myself locked onto old ideals. There are many elements of this field I thought I would never accept or believe. That is, until now. Depending on how far you, the reader, have followed my work, or even the story of Norman, you may or may not be very in tune with my train of thought.

As I have said over and over, my studies into the realm of the paranormal have always been firmly grounded in modern science. I have been extremely stubborn over the years, refusing to sway too far from measurable data. Those who know me well would tell you that I have never uttered the word "demon" in any case, and I have worked well over one thousand of them.

It has been very difficult for me to welcome anything beyond scientific research and exploration. I have to admit at this point, and I do so proudly, that not everything can be measured scientifically. I am a firm believer now that science can't answer all of the questions in our known and unknown universe. There is a reason it is called unknown.

I have been publishing my work for over a decade now for all the world to see, read, and study. I glance back on those old entries and chronicles of my paranormal investigations and see a completely different person than I am today. Growing up, I was never one to buy into magic or myth. From the beginning, I wanted to prove that all of the ghost stories had some inkling of truth behind them. I wanted to present work that validated those tales and paranormal claims.

It was one thing to say you witnessed the phenomenal and it was another to actually show someone you did. My earlier books were very cut-and-dry. They chronicled my work in the field of paranormal research, where each chapter was a different story and a different case. I read those entries now and see how stubbornly unmoved I was from keeping science behind my actions and how closed-minded I was to seeing beyond that.

I have always said I have an open mind, and you have to before even considering work in proving the afterlife, but I wasn't as open-minded as one would think. Norman came along and slowly altered my perception on just about everything I had ever studied, fought for, or tried to teach others.

It was easy for me to say that Norman was haunted. I mean, you can't witness what we did and think otherwise. It was easy to present data and have outsiders look and see that there was something more to him than just cloth and plastic. I could easily show the erratic and unpredictable temperature drops or incredible electromagnetic fields that surrounded the doll.

But the only thing that evidence proved was that something unknown to our science was controlling Norman. It didn't answer the question of how it was doing so. I couldn't lay out all of the data and say, "This is why." Logging the fields and the temperatures and coupling that with all of the photographs and videos was one thing. But actually being able to determine the cause of all of it was another. Sure, Norman could move. Sure, Norman was documented with unexplainable energy fields around him. But why? What caused all of it? That is the part our science has yet to offer up. Currently, there are no tangible methods for answering all of the questions that arose from the data gathered during all of the research with Norman, or any other paranormal case for that matter.

In 1962, something happened with that doll. Maybe if I would have been there, I could have seen it for myself or at least have a better understanding now as to why he is haunted. But I wasn't, and my work didn't start happening until five decades later.

The stories are all the same. I've seen it over and over throughout literature and television. We get the haunted part, but we never get the reasons as to why. And I am not talking about a motive or a cerebral reason for a spirit to be haunting a location or an object or a doll. I am talking about how they are able to do it. Our science stops there.

There is a world far beyond ours that has captivated the minds of millions since the beginning. There has always been the belief of something after, and the only thing that has changed is what that something after might be. I have seen enough since 1987 to securely believe that there is something beyond our own flesh and blood. I don't think we will ever truly have all of the answers until we are there to see it and understand it all for ourselves after we die.

I recently read through my first book, which was released in 2009. It was an awakening, so to speak, to realize just how different ten years can make a person. Views change. I read through it and witnessed where my mind was at that time and discovered that much of what I believed then, I do not now. And much of what I didn't believe then, I do now.

Throughout the years, I never wanted to be the guy that said I had witnessed something extraordinary and not follow that up with something of substance. I always had to have that extra piece and that extra layer of truth to go with all of my claims. I guess that is why I worked so hard on the

Norman case and let it completely take over my life. But some things are just what they are, and they don't need any further explanation.

Years ago, I would have never found myself thinking like that. Sometimes you just have to leave things be. I think I could continue researching Norman for the rest of my life and end up no further than I am right now in actually proving with concrete evidence that he is haunted. There will always be something that can be picked apart, and there will always be alternative solutions offered. But I know in my heart that Norman is truly an amazing discovery. I took the good with the bad, and so did my family just so me and Christina could continue on in hopes of finding those reasons why. I never did.

Three solid years of living that haunted doll, and although some might argue that I have in my possession some amazing and credible evidence in favor of his paranormal being, I don't have anything that explains how any of that was even possible. And what I mean by that is I don't have anything that I could present to a scientific community that could be analyzed and reveal beyond a shadow of a doubt that Norman is haunted. But do I really need it? With all that my family and I have seen, what does it really matter in the end?

I have to put my ego aside and accept the fact that I will never be able to explain how that doll can do what it does. I'm certain I could spend the next few years continuing on with him and have more video and photographs and more strange temperature changes and electromagnetic fields. But why? There comes a point when you have to realize that until we can offer up something else that goes beyond the typical scientific method, we will find ourselves simply regurgitating the same data over and over. We need new and better methods of measurement to advance the data we gather in this field. All of the current techniques have brought us to a wall—answers are on the other side, and we have no way of getting to them.

Maybe one day I will learn more about the history of the doll and maybe more will be revealed to me concerning why he does what he does. But all that will do is bring to the table more words and more stories. I have to accept that now, and I do. I think I would drive myself crazy going too much further with him.

I have done everything imaginable and conducted every test imaginable to prove that our haunted doll is something not of this earth. There is no question about that. Norman is haunted, and he haunted us over and over and over. Admitting that I can't take this any further is very difficult for me to do.

I am very grateful that Norman fell into our laps years ago, even if it was entirely by chance. He came just at the right time for me. Having worked all of the cases in the past, things were becoming beyond redundant. It was always the same old story with the same old data with the same old lingering questions dangling behind. All that ever changed were the faces that claimed it and the places that made it.

I think now, in 2019, I have become a better paranormal researcher because I have torn down the brick wall and barrier that kept me secluded to science-based exploring. I am more open now to everything and have accepted that there will always be something presented to me in which all of the questions will not be answered. So with that being said, you have to answer the questions you can, and I will continue to do so.

Maybe that is partly what makes this field so damn enticing. Maybe that is why I have spent my life living it as a career, passion, and obsession. We have yet to reach a stage in this research where there is a definitive answer for anything or where there is a person that knows it all. You can become certified in many trades or obtain degrees in various courses of study. Yet despite its social and academic acceptance, paranormal research has yet to become scientifically recognized.

This is because academic acceptance allows for the appreciation of and respect for paranormal research because it focuses on independent research. It doesn't have to be scientifically based to be impressive or even taught academically. Philosophy is a great example. That study is accepted academically but cannot be scientifically accepted. Scientific recognition requires work to fall within the realms of exact or natural sciences. Currently, paranormal research isn't an exact science nor is it natural, as it is difficult to prove or replicate. Until all of the gathered data turns into infallible information, paranormal study will remain unrecognized scientifically. We must press on until the "why" questions are answered and the "hows" become common knowledge.

Science taught me one very important thing that still sticks with me today and honestly became the root of all my work. Energy is infinite. This we know. This is a cold, hard fact. There is no denying it.

I believe that fact holds the answer to not just what is going on with Norman, but everything from the paranormal field. I have talked about this a lot in the past. Our bodies are of a bio-electrical make up. That, too, is a fact.

To put it simply, when we die, that electricity, that energy, goes somewhere.

Some believe that energy is a soul that ascends to the heavens or falls to hell. Others, like me, believe that it floats on a plane of existence we don't pay enough attention to. I mean really, think about that. When you die, your energy leaves the body and begins its immortal and infinite journey throughout our earth.

Think about how many living things have died since the beginning of time. Now think about how much energy must be out there just floating around, moving between one another, and swirling around us at any given time. That number is astronomical.

Energy does not die; that is a fact. Energy simply changes form. That, too, is a fact. That is the part of science that has fueled me since I first began looking for the reasons paranormal phenomena are possible. That energy, our energy, is the reason. But after that, we are presented with endless questions of how it works, why it works, and why it sometimes acts differently. It certainly explains how it is very possible for us to continue to get glimpses of deceased loved ones. They are still there. They simply changed form.

Whatever energy stopped and took over an innocent-looking doll back in 1962 certainly wasn't a positive energy. I can only speculate. As I alluded to earlier, maybe that energy came from a baby who never truly lived. Maybe the energy that planted itself inside of Norman came from a person who once lived and was evil in life. After all, what would a rapist or a murderer be in the afterlife? Don't you think they would be much of the same, only maybe with a few attributes we have yet to understand? That's why there are stories of good ghosts and that's why there are stories of bad ghosts. They all were once people. The good, the bad, and everything in between. Either way, no matter the true origin, Norman is evil.

So I believe that whatever possessed Norman all of those decades ago came with sinister intent and he, she, or it is firmly comfortable in its shell. Coming to these conclusions and rediscovering myself has helped me decide where to go from here when it came to the haunted doll. I knew deep down I didn't want to see it go, but again, how much longer could I keep documenting the same material over and over?

How much longer would it go on before luck wasn't on my side and the anger and evil inside of him became too powerful for us to handle anymore? We consider ourselves lucky so far. A lot of crazy occurrences have been documented and experienced by myself, my family, research colleagues, and friends.

Unfortunately, a lot of those occurrences did not come without pain and suffering, so I paid a price and continued to. And I would continue to, as long as I kept him and kept traveling down the road I was.

I have grown as a paranormal researcher and now I can honestly say that I have lived and researched firsthand the phenomenon known as "haunted objects." I look back on the past three years, and it feels like it could easily have been ten. The hardest part for me at this point was deciding on where to go from here as far as the doll was concerned. He had changed my views and even changed my research to a degree. I guess in many ways I should be thanking him. But I don't think his intent was opening my mind up to rare and unquestionable phenomena.

Whatever his motive, whatever his intent, the doll always resorted back to something evil. His pattern was predictable at this point. That certainly raised some concern.

I had one seemingly simple yet horrific question branded in my brain. What if Norman changes the tide during an investigation involving a malevolent spirit? Which led to more and more questions. What if Norman wasn't really exhibiting his entire power this whole time? What if he held all of the cards this entire time? Memories occasionally reminded me what capacity he holds, and it's never in my favor.

With a clear head, I decided that wasn't a chance I was willing to take anymore. Considering how useful and powerful he was as a tool during on-site research, what if he teamed up with or absorbed yet another evil entity? That sounds ludicrous, but all bets were off when it came to him. I'm open to anything, and I think it is best to be prepared.

So I had to make a very important and concise decision.

We once felt at ease when he needed to be locked away. We have done that twice now. Once with his own room and once with a glass coffin. But was I going to allow our guard to remain down for him to slowly and strategically take advantage of us again? As calm as things were, and as productive as our investigations were becoming, it was easy to keep on running down that path. I think he knew that. I kept feeling like we were following his lead instead of mine, and that left me sitting very uncomfortably. I had to make a decision that would change everything. I had to decide if what we were currently doing was the right thing. I did not leave this to a family discussion. I did not even tell Christina what conclusion I had come to. It was time to bury him for good and put him to rest in a place less travelled by.

It was time to move on. I knew I had to. I knew Christina wanted to. But when you are dealing with something you can't truly explain, how does one actually go about that?

17

The Secret

Norman was a hard case to crack. On one hand, he made multiple attempts to kill me and even more attempts to shock and terrorize us. On the other hand, he became a staple in our investigative work by aiding us in direct spiritual communication.

You are probably asking the same questions I asked. How? Why? Can he be trusted? I can't say for sure, but maybe bringing him into the field of paranormal research satisfied some undying desire of his. He was certainly the center of attention now. It was certainly noticeable when the activity decreased at our home. It nearly stopped just short of us taking him on the road with us to investigations, starting with the old Packhouse.

Yet that certainly didn't stop him from attacking Christina or continuing on with his haunting ways. He just wasn't as in my face about it. Norman was like my yin and yang. He had become my good and my evil. When left in our home like some sort of sideshow, he wreaks havoc. When working with us in the field of paranormal research, he exhibits helpfulness.

That last sentence was very difficult to say because honestly it sounds completely ridiculous. A veteran paranormal researcher rooted firmly in science using a haunted doll to conduct investigative work is not something I would have ever correlated with me. Yet here I am.

Was this the end? Was this going to be life with Norman from here on out? Those were questions I asked myself every time we loaded him into that old antique trunk and drove off into the paranormal sunset toward an investigation. Believe me when I tell you I have thought a thousand times over what will happen if he changes sides again and becomes a full on enemy of the family.

After the first book, and especially after the *A Haunting* episode, I probably received well over ten thousand emails offering advice on Norman.

I was happy and grateful to receive such a response. While some correspondents were pointing and waving their fingers and saying, "What you're doing is wrong," others were supportive and offered up wisdom on the subject. Many discussed spiritual binding techniques while others suggested simply burying him.

I tried to respond to as many as possible, and I did, for the most part, to those who actually came to the table with a solution over something ridiculous like giving up Norman to somebody who is on television. Yes, that's true. Many people said I should give him to a professional paranormal television star. I had to laugh at that, and I still do. But it wasn't their fault for thinking like that. All they had seen was the story on *A Haunting*, so they had no clue of my hisory in the field.

However, I do thank those who reached out, who took the time to learn everything concerning Norman and myself. He doesn't belong in a haunted museum some-where, folks. That was the most irresponsible suggestion I have heard to date. Placing Norman in a situation where a countless amount of visitors could come into contact with him would be dangerous. But I did take many suggestions to heart, and some of those aided me in the decision to bury Norman and everything that came with him.

This wasn't a decision I made overnight. It took a lot of thought and planning. This was literally a top-secret project that nobody, not even my wife, could know about before it was carried out. There was a little bit of worry in the back of my head that he may try to stop me, but he didn't.

I utilized maps to find the perfect, isolated location to entomb him. It was very important as well that the location was easily accessible to me for routine checks after the fact. So when initiating the plan, and for any events thereafter, I needed total anonymity. All events required covert tactics. I needed to make sure that nobody saw me go in or out of the location … ever. The spot I had finally chosen was perfect.

I located what would be his burial site about six miles away from any civilization in either direction. It took me an hour from our home to find the perfect location. I parked at the tree line of Norman's resting spot, which was six miles further from there. So I am sure you can guess, even without me telling you, that the area was deep in the woods of North Carolina.

About sixty percent of the state is covered in uninhabited forest.[4] The best I can say is good luck trying to find him. Although I really wouldn't try to for your own sake. You know what will happen, and that, my friends, is a terrifying responsibility. He will haunt you.

I wasn't happy about having to drive, but I had no choice. So I took our truck, a trailer with an all-terrain vehicle (ATV) on it, along with all of the tools I would need to see the task through. I brought a shovel, a powder mix for concrete, and gallons of water. Luckily for me, our ATV had a rack on the back, which made transporting all of the supplies and Norman much easier across the thick-wooded and swamp-infested region.

---

4. Mark Megalos, Rick Hamilton, and Colby Lambert, "Forest Land Enhancement Practices in North Carolina," NC State Extension Publications. N.C. Cooperative Extension, January 18, 2019, "https://content.ces.ncsu.edu/forest-land-enhancement-practices-in-north-carolina.

Doing this by foot was simply not an option. It would have taken me a couple of days to complete my mission considering the weight of everything I needed. I had to be as quick as possible so as not to draw any attention for the sake of the passersby and my wife.

It was five thirty in the morning on September 21, 2019, when I began my trek back through the dark forest. After dodging tree branches and having near misses with rocky terrain, I arrived at the chosen spot just before eleven in the morning. I chose a spot secluded and surrounded by swampland.

The first thing I did was dig a deep hole about ten yards from the neighboring swamp. I dug a two-foot by two-foot hole. Of course, the entire time I had to keep my eye out for any dangerous wildlife. I mean, after all, I was in a place nobody knew about, and furthermore, no one knew I was even there. If something had attacked and killed me, I would have been laid to rest alongside Norman, and nobody would have ever known.

Wouldn't that have been poetic?

After I finished digging, I poured about six-inches worth of the concrete mix into the hole. I then grabbed Norman, who was now back in his glass coffin, and placed him on top of the first layer of concrete. I filled the majority of the hole, about six inches from the surface, with the remainder of the concrete mix. Then I proceeded to use a little garden shovel to blend the water with the mix to its desired form.

I sat for about an hour before topping the hole off with dirt. I made it as if nobody was ever there. I did not place a marker of any kind to accompany his resting place. The last thing I wanted was somebody to stumble upon it—let alone recognize it—and dig him up. It certainly was not going to be easy for a person to discover him, let alone pull that concrete block out of the hole. Your average person could not tote an estimated three-hundred-pound object out of the woods. At least not without a ton of help and resources.

My plan was airtight. Nobody was ever going to find this, let alone even know what they had found. For all intents and purposes, it's just a concrete block in the ground. It isn't like a person would even know that something is inside the concrete block let alone that something being a baleful haunted doll.

After documenting the entire situation in my journal, it started to rain. The rain was symbolic in a way. It reminded me of somberness. It reminded me of tears and farewells. I stood for a moment over his unmarked grave, just thinking about the past three years. Burying such an important part of our life came with an overwhelming feeling of joy and closure. I mean, how the hell could Norman haunt us now? Sure, the memory remained, and his ghosts were far from gone, but to us, a chapter came to a close.

I snapped out of my joyous mourning that morning and packed up my gear to head home.

I raced back through the dark wood, and six hours later, I found my truck. It certainly payed off being a Boy Scout. I loaded the ATV back onto the trailer, jumped in the truck, and headed back to the house. The hour drive gave me plenty of time to think about how I was going to tell Christina about what I had done.

Honestly, it went over better than I expected.

I returned home and finally told Christina what I had done and where I had been. I wouldn't tell her the exact location, and at first that really upset her. I assured her that what I had done was right. After some further explaining and convincing, my wife decided to accept fate. She is quite accustomed to secrecy when it comes to cases of utmost priority. In this line of work, confidentiality and undisclosed cases are the norm. Eventually, she understood that it would remain a secret that would follow me to my grave. It goes without saying that a level of comfort fell upon her. No more worries about fires, flying objects, threatening messages, and harm.

Hell, it felt good just typing that out.

Now I think about years and years into the future. Maybe one day a highway with cars flying by will be over top of Norman. All of those people zipping by without a clue as to the evil resting beneath them. Maybe something commercial will be built there. Maybe somebody will build a home. Regardless of what happens in the future, Norman will be there.

I can't convince myself that his resting place will remain. Commercial development of land happens every day. But for now, he is pretty far away from ever seeing that. And if that concrete block is discovered and discarded, Norman will be in a place I won't even be aware of. Maybe the future will bring just that, so I can die knowing that he is lost forever.

Afterword

To this day, nobody has come forward stating they were the original owner of Norman.

There is still a story out there to tell about a young girl who lost everything and grew up with a haunted doll tormenting her life for fifty-odd years. Considering what my family experienced, I have to believe she was haunted by him too. Maybe not to the extent we were, but I think she knew. I would love to tell that story. I can only imagine the lifetime worth of stories she could share.

Despite the many attempts we have made to locate his original owner, nothing concrete has solidified. She could be dead at this point for all we know. But certainly someone, somewhere, knows what really happened that Christmas Eve in 1968. Somebody has to know where five decades of Norman went.

Years ago, when we first acquired Norman from the antique shop, the old lady running the place told us of the fire, and the death, and the lonely, little girl left with only the doll. The old woman at the shop is long gone, so reaching into her brain further than we already have is out of the question. I want to believe that maybe she was the one all along.

There are definitely many questions left unanswered. This doll was hidden in that box for a reason yet was trusted to me.

Norman has taught me a lot about life. Any of us at any time can be a victim of something our science has yet to truly solidify. Science doesn't explain everything, and it never will. I never thought there would be a point in my life where I actually agreed with that statement. But I guess even though my roots are firmly planted in the scientific exploration of the paranormal, I am still grounded enough to realize it can't answer everything.

It is comforting to know there are others out there that can share in these experiences. For the majority of my life, I sought out those who experienced just that. But my own personal hell has proven no one is immune. I have to accept that, and I have to keep sharing—come what may. Norman was born to haunt, and I was born to be haunted.

I have walked away from this experience with a refreshing sense of purpose. Nothing is ever truly gone. Thinking like that will definitely make you a better field researcher, if that's what you want to be. It isn't always bells and whistles, pretty lights, and electromagnetic this and that. There is a humanistic side that is often missed.

I'm sure at some point in your life you have been told to never look back. In this field, that is all you do. You have to. You know what I have experienced for the past two decades if you followed along with my career, but there is a man behind all of that. I am not a character in a book, and neither is that damned doll. I am a real person, and Norman is a real entity.

As I said early on in this book, a true ghost story has no ending. That was not said for dramatic purposes. I will continue to document. If not Norman, it will always be something else.

With Norman put to rest, I am actively working undisclosed cases and doing research, which is publicly accessible on my website. Much of what I am actively doing is made public for all the world to see through my videos and blogs. It is refreshing to wake up every day to new cases and new beginnings with somebody's ghost. Norman had become so much a part of our lives over the years that I had forgotten what it was like to be fully immersed in the everyday field of paranormal research. It was like I had taken an extended vacation from client cases while focusing on the doll. Now

I am back to my normal paranormal life of handling mysteries and hauntings for others.

I am one of the few that is blessed, and I have been for well over two decades. I've been a professional phenomenologist researching paranormal claims day in and day out. Not many people can say that line of work is beyond a hobby to them. I am very fortunate in that respect. I get to research and report and put it out there for all the world to see.

I have a new lease on life knowing that such a darkness existed. That means there is a lot of light out there as well, and it further proves that there is a life after we die.

I want you to know I am easily accessible. I want you to know who I am. I want you to see the passion I live every day. I hope to continue to share my fieldwork with you through literary works and other mediums.

Could this be the end of the Norman saga? It very well could be. I was ready to put him to rest and I did. Right now, we are at peace.

If Norman ends up in the hands of somebody else in the future, hopefully my books will act as a helpful guide. I don't want some innocent person starting from scratch with him like we did. Other than my occasional visit to make sure he is still where I left him, Norman is gone and beyond our control. Part of my heart feels sympathetic while the other part feels fear and relief at the same time.

We have raised hell, and just like our mortal lives, it came to an end eventually—or at least as close to an end as you can come. After all of this, I will never forget what he has done to me and my family.

When I walked away from that grave site, I came back, and I came back haunted with the memories of that doll. I came back haunted from that antique shop years ago where I first picked him up. Now I was walking away from the area I last put him down.

There is still so much more to discover in the world of phenomenology. There will always be new cases, fresh experiences, and discoveries within the realm of paranormal research. Norman isn't just a case or a file now. I will be talking about that doll for years to come, I suppose, but I'm not going to let it dictate my life.

I thought when I shifted my focus entirely to Norman that I had given up why I started in this field to being with, when in fact, I simply added a hot file, a new story, and a glimpse of hope that one day we will have all of the answers. This is definitely the most elaborate, evidence-producing, curious, and satisfying case in my catalog. Where I go from here is all dictated by the ghosts. I don't think about what tomorrow will bring forth. I deliberate about what was left behind yesterday. That determines my tomorrow.

To my readers, thank you for lending your insight and showing such a great interest in my family's demon. To Norman, I say goodbye.

Bibliography

Lancaster, Stephen. "Activity at our house has been on the rise ever since we started collecting haunted objects." Facebook, July 26, 2016. https://www.facebook.com/wraithwrite /posts/1580550655578507.

Lancaster, Stephen and Monstervisiontv. "Norman the \Haunted Doll AMAZING Investigation 2019." Facebook. Video. February 1, 2019. https://www.facebook .com/monsterVisionTV/videos/603190670123645/.

Megalos, Mark, Rick Hamilton, and Colby Lambert. "Forest Land Enhancement Practices in North Carolina." NC State Extension Publications. N.C. Cooperative Extension. January 18, 2019. "https://content.ces.ncsu.edu /forest-land-enhancement-practices-in-north-carolina.

To Write to the Author

If you wish to contact the author or would like more information about this book, please write to the author in care of Llewellyn Worldwide Ltd. and we will forward your request. Both the author and publisher appreciate hearing from you and learning of your enjoyment of this book and how it has helped you. Llewellyn Worldwide Ltd. cannot guarantee that every letter written to the author can be answered, but all will be forwarded. Please write to:

Stephen Lancaster
℅ Llewellyn Worldwide
2143 Wooddale Drive
Woodbury, MN 55125-2989

Please enclose a self-addressed stamped envelope for reply,
or $1.00 to cover costs. If outside the U.S.A., enclose
an international postal reply coupon.

Many of Llewellyn's authors have websites with additional information and resources. For more information, please visit our website at http://www.llewellyn.com